*Gardening with Native Plants
in the Upper Midwest*

A BUR OAK GUIDE

Holly Carver, series editor

Gardening with Native Plants in the Upper Midwest

Bringing the Tallgrass Prairie Home

Judy Nauseef

UNIVERSITY OF IOWA PRESS
IOWA CITY

University of Iowa Press, Iowa City 52242
Copyright © 2016 by the University of Iowa Press
www.uiowapress.org
Printed in the United States of America
Photos copyright © 2016 by the author unless otherwise noted.
All other photos copyright © by their photographers.
Design by Kristina Kachele Design, llc

Library of Congress Cataloging-in-Publication Data
Nauseef, Judy, author.
Gardening with native plants in the Upper Midwest :
bringing the tallgrass prairie home / Judy Nauseef.
pages   cm. — (Bur Oak Guides)
Includes bibliographical references and index.
ISBN 978-1-60938-407-4 (pbk), ISBN 978-1-60938-408-1 (ebk)
1. Native plant gardening—Middle West.
2. Endemic plants—Middle West.   3. Landscape gardening—Middle West.
I. Title.   II. Series: Bur Oak guide.
SB439.N45   2016
635.9'5177—dc23   2015028381

Dedicated to my father,
Abraham Nathaniel Barnett,
who taught me scholarship

Contents

Acknowledgments

I am especially grateful to three Iowans who accepted me without judgment into the community of native plant enthusiasts and shared their knowledge with me. I have learned and continue to learn about native plants, their history, and how to assure that future generations will know them. These people include Chris Henze, Johnson County roadside vegetation manager; Cornelia F. Mutel, historian and archivist for IIHR-Hydroscience and Engineering at the University of Iowa College of Engineering; and the late Robert Sayre, author and professor of English at the University of Iowa.

I thank the contributing photographers for their generosity and enthusiasm for the book: Jason Allen, Country Landscapes, Inc.; Roy Diblik, Northwind Perennial Farm; Neil Diboll, Prairie Nursery; Deborah Groat; Margaret Kiekhaefer; Mark Müller; Douglas Owens-Pike, EnergyScapes; Jack Pizzo, Pizzo and Associates, Ltd.; Salsbury-Schweyer, Inc.; and Adam Woodruff, Adam Woodruff + Associates. I also thank my clients, who put their trust in me, and the contractor RVM Landscaping, who for the last few years has installed most of my landscapes. I rely on Rodney Von Muenster's advice and appreciate his willingness to learn about native landscaping. I truly appreciate that my editor Holly Carver recognized me as both a professional landscape designer and writer, giving me the opportunity to write this book.

My parents, husband, sister, and children, as always, have supported my work even when it did not fit into the category of "normal employment."

Preface

In my work as a professional landscape designer, I search for inspiration from many sources. Starting with houseplants in my first apartment, adding trees and shrubs to later yards, and finally discovering perennials, I developed a love of plants. This love provided the spark when I began designing. Over time, how people actually use their gardens became more important to me and helped define my role. Eventually, the prairie landscape came into my view through verbal and written descriptions and visits to reconstructed prairies. I definitely was inspired. I had a new tool for creating landscapes that suit the homeowner and at the same time spread the word about native plants.

I began to learn about an entirely new palette of plants and landforms. I planted some prairie plant plugs in a former vegetable bed and many years later am still enjoying the vibrant community of plants, birds, butterflies, and insects. In Iowa, while serving on the Integrated Roadside Vegetation Management Committee for Johnson County, I learned a tremendous amount and realized that there were people in my community with an incredible knowledge of and commitment to native plants. As a landscape designer, I wanted to bring an understanding of the native plant community to my work.

As in any new endeavor, this process has taken time to learn, and it still continues for me. The idea of using native plants in gardens is relatively new, and information on how to garden in this way is lacking. You will find encyclopedic books on native plants that offer valuable horticultural information but not always information on which insects use which plant as a food source or on how certain plants will perform in your garden. Some of these books include North American plants, not just midwestern natives. Some include cultivars of native plants. Some are simply beautiful and may inspire but do not instruct.

I looked for ways to incorporate this new inspiration into my design work. Although my library grew and grew, it still did not include the book I needed. That book would discuss making native plants part of a designed garden and using native plants to create an outdoor space for homeowners to enjoy. It would help me decide how to replace problematic nonnative plants with native plants that would attract pollinators. It would provide examples of well-designed landscapes where native plants enhance paths, patios, pergolas, and steps. Maybe most important, it would be relevant to the Upper Midwest.

While serving on the Bur Oak Land Trust (formerly the Johnson County Heritage Trust) board of directors, I met even more people with a wealth of knowledge about conservation. One of them, Holly Carver, a series editor at the University of Iowa Press, also served on the board, and during a brief conversation we both expressed the need for the same book, the one I needed but had yet to find. Hence, this book began.

The better landscape designers, I believe, are also gardeners. I began to become a gardener while living in New York State in an apartment in an old house owned by a lovely elderly woman and her kind and generous husband. They let my husband and me use part of their yard for a garden as well as their garage to store our bikes. I knew nothing about gardening, and my landlady gave me some starter information. She composted leaves at the bottom of the yard, my introduction to organic matter. I began to read all I could about vegetable gardening. A couple of years later in Madison, Wisconsin, we planted our first large garden in the Midwest, a rented plot in a community garden. Successes in that early garden led us to grow vegetables after each move. Upon returning to the Midwest for what has turned into a stay of over thirty years, we added trees, shrubs, perennials, and fruits to our landscapes.

Through gardening I learned about landscape design. I returned to school, attending Kirkwood Community College in Cedar Rapids, Iowa, to earn a degree in horticulture and landscape design. As a working artist I was comfortable with the idea of learning landscape design. The study of horticulture would fill in very large gaps in my knowledge. I had studied literature and art in college and then communications in graduate school. Working for a graphic design firm and then two nonprofit professional organizations in their publications departments and finally as a fine artist provided a wonderful background for garden design and writing.

For over twenty-five years I have worked as a landscape designer, continuing my education through attending workshops and symposia, reading books and magazines, and visiting many gardens. Talking with other landscape designers and contractors has proved indispensable. Gaining expertise, I became an Iowa Certified Nurseryman (now Iowa Certified Nursery Professional) in 1997 and a Certified Member of the Association of Professional Landscape Designers (APLD) in 1996. Both certifications have required continuing education. APLD gave me a community in which to learn and grow. I served on the board of directors as chair of the certification committee and in 2009 as president. I am now a fellow of the organization.

I write all of this not to create an intimidating view of myself as an author. Certainly, I continue to learn, make mistakes, change my ideas, and realize my limitations. The purpose is to demonstrate that I have worked to develop the ability to critique and assess the landscapes I see every day and to find solutions to those that do not work for us or for our environment.

As you read this book, I will share with you the sources I have used to arrive at this point, which is only one place along the way. Hopefully, there will be more and better places as I continue to garden, design, read, and write.

In chapter 1, I make the case for gardening with native plants and doing so with a plan. As a gardener I know the joys of visiting nurseries and wandering their rows. The colors, textures, smells, puddles of irrigation water, and those shallow cardboard boxes urge us to create a beautiful garden in our landscape. But I see nothing sadder than a once-vibrant plant sitting next to the garage, failing a bit more each day simply because someone had not planned adequately for its arrival. I encourage homeowners to become familiar with the skills of a landscape designer or to hire one so their chance of success will be higher.

In chapter 2, I explain how I was introduced to the midwestern landscape, and I review the Midwest's geological past and the movement of settlers west into the plains states. After we moved to Iowa, I began reading about the prairie landscape that used to cover the state along with savannas and woodlands. I became intrigued with what I would have seen on my ordinary residential lot on the eastern edge of Iowa City. I had gardened without thinking about which plants were native to Iowa and had been drawn into the world of endless varieties of ornamental plants. Eventually, I realized I could bring some of the prairie into my yard.

Chapter 3 makes a more thorough case for gardening with native plants. The condition of our environment, more than creating beauty and evoking the landforms of the past, calls us to act. Here, I also include writings of experts who have helped me form my thoughts and ideas on the topic. I have found that by bringing biodiversity into my garden, I can make a difference. The habitat I create in my garden provides a place where ecological balance returns. Starting on a small scale is possible.

Chapter 4 describes the basic process for planning and designing your garden. I include sources that offer further details. There are many books on landscape design. As a landscape designer, my goal is to create a garden that will bring the homeowners outside. The outdoor spaces need to be comfortable. The design will solve problems of lack of screening, soggy areas, or too much or too little shade or sun. It may add patios and pergolas for entertaining or solitary relaxing. The designed landscape can enable homeowners to begin to live sustainably on their land. This chapter includes photos of garden projects in which the plant palette includes native plants. I have asked gardeners and designers around the Midwest to allow me to use their photos of gardens designed with native plants. Some of these people are old friends, but many are new friends, and all are excited about this book. They are ecologists, landscape architects and designers, master gardeners, landscape contractors, teachers, and gardeners. They feel strongly that we must conserve and improve our environment.

Chapter 5 includes photos showing plant combinations to provide examples of what is possible when using native plants in your garden. Some photos have both native and nonnative plants to illustrate how native plants can be added to an existing garden. I know of gardeners who have ripped out their nonnative gardens to begin anew with a native garden, but this does not work for everyone. I would like to see more attempts to create diverse gardens. That is where an improved environment will begin.

Chapter 6 illustrates residential prairies. Some are on city or suburban lots, and some are on acreages. These are landscapes where the homeowners wanted to plant prairies. They have ordered local ecotype seed from a regional seed source and chosen seed mixtures to suit their needs. The photos of these landscapes show wonderful results in Wisconsin, Illinois, and Iowa.

Chapter 7 provides information on garden planting and maintenance, practices I have developed after many years of gardening. It includes methods of planting and maintaining native plants and prairies I have learned from midwestern experts. The resources at the back of this book list outstanding publications on this topic as well as the many excellent sources I used during my research and writing. It also includes seed and plant sources, organizations, Internet publications, governmental sources, and public arboretum and prairie sites. The scientific names for plants follow the International Code of Botanical Nomenclature.

The book includes "Upper Midwest" in its title for a reason. The information about creating a garden with native plants applies to a large area. For those living in Iowa; in much of Illinois and Missouri; and in parts of Minnesota, Wisconsin, North Dakota, South Dakota, Nebraska, Kansas, Indiana, Michigan, and Ohio, their heritage is tied to the tallgrass prairie.

This book can be many things to different people. It is an introduction to the prairie landscape and to a nearly century-long movement to restore prairie to the Midwest. It explains how we can use native plants in our own personal landscapes and as a result bring a diversity of plants, insects, and birds into our neighborhoods. It illustrates how understanding and following basic landscape design principles can lead to successful gardens. The purpose of this book is to help gardeners decide how to use native plants in the design of their gardens.

*Gardening with Native Plants
in the Upper Midwest*

Native Plants and the Landscape

Gardeners continually search for opportunities to make their gardens more interesting, beautiful, and productive. The many magazines and books selling off the shelves with the word "garden" or "gardening" in their titles show that this is true. The landscape sections of Internet sites Pinterest and Houzz have thousands of users. Shoppers look for new styles or plants to make their gardens special. Now, native plants bring those possibilities to the gardener. For a landscape designer, native prairie, woodland, and wetland plants bring exciting options and solutions to design projects.

Native Plants

Our native species are "those that were long-term members of the Midwest's original prairies, woodlands, bottomland forests, and wetlands," according to ecologist and writer Cornelia F. Mutel. I like Mutel's definition because it is simple, and for those involved in the restoration of woodlands and prairies it works well. The discussion of native plants continues in the community of ecologists, designers, and others. In addition, in the Midwest, despite the predominance of agricultural land, the idea of what is native is not complicated. Illinois landscape architect and ecologist Jack Pizzo defines a native plant as an indigenous species that is normally found in a part of a particular ecosystem. These are straightforward definitions that work well in the Midwest. A definition from Dick Darke and Doug Tallamy in their book *The Living Landscape* emphasizes a plant's functionality: "a plant or animal that has evolved in a given place over a period of time sufficient to develop complex and essential relationships with the physical environment and other organisms in a given ecological community." They write with familiarity of the eastern United States and its large areas of forest.

Not surprisingly, for the gardener and designer, these definitions seem hard to apply. We are choosing plants for gardens and hoping to attract bees and butterflies, but we do not really have a functioning ecosystem. We are often starting with a few square feet or a few square yards. Pizzo reassures us that every little bit counts even though a native landscape horizon to horizon may be the goal. Just getting started is the key. Designer and writer C. Colston Burrell explains that native plants need an ecological niche; they need to have a context. We sometimes have to construct that context. We can do this with a well-planned design (photo 1).

In my home landscape, I have the luxury of space to experiment with many kinds of plants and to develop designed gardens over time. When I work with clients, my role includes creating a garden that will work for them. When they come to me requesting a native garden, my job is clear. Without this directive, I look for ways to include native plants and to design with a concern for conserving resources.

Gardeners are known for finding a plant they must have, bringing it home, and wandering around the yard looking for a place to plant it or sticking it in the first available spot they see. This happens with all kinds of plants: annuals, perennials, shrubs, and trees. And now it is happening with native plants as they have shown up in garden centers

1. Little bluestem (*Schizachyrium scoparium*), Goldsturm black-eyed Susan (*Rudbeckia fulgida* 'Goldsturm'), purple coneflower (*Echinacea purpurea*), and Peter Pan goldenrod (*Solidago* 'Peter Pan') enhance a perennial garden.

and catalogs. Even as the chance to add beauty to their yards fuels the acquisition of more and more plants, gardeners should learn about a plant's needs and habits and make a plan before purchasing anything. My goal is to help the consumer choose each native plant carefully and prepare for its arrival.

Gardeners in the Upper Midwest have challenges to meet. The growing season is short, winters are cold, and summers are hot. Snow cover may or may not be adequate to protect plants from freezing and thawing patterns. Ice storms and tornados occur every year. More recent challenges have appeared. A growing deer population, new pests, more frequent flooding and drought, and more extreme temperatures add to the stress of the garden and the gardener.

2. New England aster (*Symphyotrichum novae-angliae*) and side oats grama (*Bouteloua curtipendula*) glow in the autumn prairie.

Native plants are new, well not really new, tools to meet these challenges (photo 2). They developed over centuries and in the process created the most fertile soils on the planet. These tallgrass prairie plants' roots grew many feet into the ground, making it friable and nutrient rich as roots decomposed. In addition to the well-known benefits of living in the Midwest—friendly people, clean air, hopefully improving water quality, good schools—the legacy of the tallgrass prairie enriches our lives if we will recognize it. The term "sense of place" may be overused now by garden designers, but it means a gardener recognizes that native plants naturally belong in gardens. It is similar to how vintners describe their wine, as tasting of the land on which the grapes were grown.

Numerous books and other resources are available on the history of the tallgrass prairie, prairie restoration, planting new prairies, prairie management, and sustainable landscape practices. There are many books of native plant descriptions, which are included in the resources at the back of this book.

Sustainability

In addition to being a tool for the gardener to achieve beautiful and thriving gardens, native plants in a landscape will make it better for humans and other animals and insects that inhabit our world. These plants help keep rainwater on-site, which reduces runoff into lakes and streams. They attract insects that feed on them and create cover for birds and beneficial insects. They reduce maintenance by decreasing the need for watering and weeding. The garden becomes a lively place where we work and play. The benefit that native plants bring to the landscape is a diversity of plants, insects, butterflies and dragonflies, frogs and toads, turtles and snakes, and small mammals and a gradually improving soil.

The subject here is really sustainability, possibly an overused word with no clear meaning. However, looking at the work of the Sustainable Sites Initiative, we find ideas and a framework for action. This collaboration between the Lady Bird Johnson Wildflower Center, the United States Botanic Garden, and the American Society of Landscape Architects in conjunction with a diverse group of technical advisers and stakeholder organizations developed a rating system and reference guide similar to the LEED (Leadership in Energy and Environmental Design) ratings for buildings. According to the Sustainable Sites Initiative website, "The central message of the Sustainable Sites Initiative program is that any landscape—whether the site of a large subdivision, a shopping mall, a park, an abandoned rail yard, or even one home—holds the potential both to improve and to regenerate the natural benefits and services provided by ecosystems in their undeveloped state." Gardeners and landscape designers are part of this movement.

Native Plants in Gardens

The process of learning about gardening with native plants includes becoming familiar with the history of where we live, how our communities came to exist, and how we can enrich our environment. You may aim for a totally native garden, but your first step is to become familiar with how to use native plants. Incorporate native plants into your existing garden or a plan for a new garden. In many situations combining native and nonnative (also known as exotic) plants enhances both. But beware: Certain exotics are known to be invasive in the Upper Midwest. Avoid using those plants. Invasive plants spread through their roots and seeds, smothering native plants and destroying habitat. Some exotics may require more water or pesticides than we are willing to use.

Even native plants suit some areas better than others. They may be aggressive, meaning they grow quickly and use all available space, overwhelming their neighbors. These are not a wise choice for planting in a garden. They are appropriate for areas of prairie or disturbed ground, or match them with plants with similar growth habits. Native plants work well in poor soils, such as those around newly constructed homes. Garden soils tend to be rich with nutrients that the gardener has added, and for some native plants this is too much and they will flop. Learning about their preferences and needs will help you create a successful garden.

Garden designers assess sites by looking at their problems and possibilities. In areas of high deer populations, we look for deer-resistant plants. In exposed, cold, sunny areas, we look for exceptionally hardy plants. Many native plants fall into both of these categories. Some tried-and-true nonnative plants such as lilacs and peonies fit into this category as well. These plants evoke old farmsteads representing hardy, persevering families. They have a place in our gardens today. Landscape architect Jens Jensen advocated the use of native plants based on his observation of what grew best in the areas where he worked. He recognized that certain plants such as lilacs and peonies held important associations in gardeners' lives. Frank Waugh wrote in 1917 that landscape architects when designing in the natural style used many indigenous species but did not exclude "the common lilac and homely apple tree." He calls the natural style a fundamental garden form. This style is dependent on the native landscape.

3. A prairie and a hayfield exist side by side in the Iowa landscape.

The agricultural landscape that surrounds us has its beauty as well. The fields lie on the same contours and horizons that held the prairies. The farmyards, farm buildings, and fields are my borrowed views today (photo 3). There is a rich resource of shapes, colors, texture, and line for the designer to use. Waugh writes, "This agricultural landscape, however, has an effective appeal of its own. It is not unfair to say that it is quite as beautiful as the native landscape which it has supplanted." Today we know that the loss of the native landscape has had a deleterious effect on the environment. We have lost more than the beauty of the prairie.

Bringing native plants back into the landscape is one way to help restore our damaged environment while at the same time creating gardens where we will spend time with our families. From my point of view, this presents a perfect opportunity to improve and enrich our community and our own lives.

2

Some History of the Midwestern Landscape

In preparing to write this book on using native plants in gardens, I have been reading and rereading many sources. Understanding the historical context of the midwestern prairie has helped me define the form of the book. Soon after I moved to Iowa in 1983, I bought and read John Madson's *Where the Sky Began*. His book was my introduction to the prairie and the landscape that once was and is no more, except in tiny remnants scattered around the state. The sense of loss Madson conveyed has stayed with me. Many people before me have felt the same loss and have written and worked with the goal of understanding our past and improving our future. Candace Savage writes, "The more we love this place as it is, the more we feel the pain of what it so recently was." She goes on to say that it is not too late to learn to understand the natural world that affects all of us.

Explorers and Settlers

Early explorers and settlers had known the treed landscape of the eastern part of the United States. When they made their way west and crossed the Mississippi River, they were astounded by the wide, treeless expanse. The new view had a beauty not known to them before and was intimidating to many. It was beautiful and frightening at the same time, with too much sky and too much light. These explorers had known only woodlands. This response is the reverse of my slightly claustrophobic reaction when visiting areas of the East Coast after living in Iowa for over thirty years. It is the feeling of being enclosed by rather than freed by the vegetation and topography.

In 1817 George Flower wrote of reaching "the entrance into one of these beautiful and light expanses of verdure . . . the beautifully indented outlines of woods and the undulating surface of the prairie." In 1839 Judge James Hall wrote, "The scenery of the prairie is striking and never fails to cause an exclamation of surprise."

Here travelers are using the term "prairie" as a familiar name for the landscape. The early French explorers who left eastern settlements and explored land to the west and southwest used the term, which in France and Quebec meant "meadow." One of them, Louis Joliet, reported about his 1683 exploration. Expecting treeless land ravaged by fire, he found prairies where settlers would not need to spend years clearing ground but could on the day of arrival put a horse- or ox-drawn wooden plow into the ground. A French explorer in 1761 wrote of southern Wisconsin, "The grass is so very high that a man is lost amongst it." We have come to refer to this large expanse as grasslands.

Others could not become comfortable with the expanse. Charles Dickens wrote of the prairie, "It was lonely and wild, but oppressive in its barren monotony. I felt that in traversing the Prairies, I could never abandon myself to the scene." Washington Irving wrote in the late 1830s, "There is something inexpressibly lonely in the solitude of the prairie."

As settlers moved west, following the explorers, they discovered the prairies. Tallgrass prairies covered Iowa, northwestern Indiana, and the northern two-thirds of Illinois. They reached into southern and western Minnesota and eastern portions of the Dakotas and Nebraska and into Missouri. These prairies had an impact on the new inhabitants. They wondered at the brightness of the open landscape, its qualities of light and space. John Madson quotes an early journalist: "The gaiety of the prairie, its embellishments and the absence of gloom and savage wildness of the forest, all contribute to dispel the feeling of loneliness which usually creeps over the mind of the solitary traveler in the wilderness." Others reported, however, the times of monotony and dread during the winter. Living on the prairie certainly required a fair amount of fortitude.

During their progress, the settlers encountered groves of trees in Michigan and Wisconsin and northeastern Iowa. The widely spaced oaks created natural parks, known as savannas, the mostly open oak woodlands with only a few trees per acre. A traveler in the mid-1880s wrote: "Lost as I was, I could not help pausing frequently when I struck the first bur-oak opening I had ever seen, to admire its novel beauty." These transition zones between woodlands and prairies hosted a large community of plants and are a landscape feature valued greatly today. They served as summer camps for Native Americans and home sites for settlers. Settlers as they traveled west observed eastern trees becoming scarce and a new mixture of trees becoming common.

Often, though, the break between woodland and prairie was abrupt, without open groves. Madson writes that a person in ten steps "passed from one world to another, across what was probably the sharpest, clearest boundary between any of the major floristic provinces of the New World." The trees of the prairie grew along waterways and on ridges. The grassland was filled with potholes, marshes, and open lakes. The prairie land rolled and undulated.

The Prairie Style

In 1906 Jens Jensen wrote, "The meadow is the bright spot of the North, reflecting light and sunshine. It has forever become an indispensable part of the home of the North—the only place in the world where real home sentiment exists." Wilhelm Miller wrote about the prairie spirit in landscape gardening in an essay of that name in 1916, stating that the new style of the "Middle West" included landscape gardening and is founded on regional character. This regional character "grows out of the most striking peculiarity of middle-western scenery, which is the prairie," flat or gently rolling and treeless. He wrote that on the prairie you can see the whole horizon. This style of gardening fits the scenery, climate, and other conditions of the prairie. It emphasizes conservation, restoration, and repetition, with respect for the beauty of native vegetation. Miller cites Jens Jensen as the first designer who took the prairie as a "leading motive." Miller went on to write about the horizontal line as "the fundamental thing in the prairie style of architecture," giving credit to Frank Lloyd Wright. He hoped this new method of expression would spread from Michigan and Ohio to South Dakota and Kansas. This was an exciting time for architecture and landscape architecture as a prairie style developed.

Why were there so few trees on the prairie? People assumed the reason was poor soils. Any ground unable to grow trees could not be fertile. Now we know that glaciations and changing climate created the conditions for prairie. The glaciers refined soil bases that held mineral wealth. The woodlands were usually on ridges or along rivers and creeks. Jens Jensen writes about the woodlands of Illinois, "There is tenderness in the deciduous forest that the conifer forest does not possess." He disparages parks and home gardens planted with imported trees.

Geology and Climate

Reading about the history and geology of the Midwest has helped me understand the lengthy development of the tallgrass prairie. Oceans advanced and retreated across North America many times over millions of years. The surface of the continent continued to buckle and twist. Forty-five million years ago, the plains climate was subtropical. About thirty-seven million years ago, the average global temperature began to drop. The tropical forests of the North American plains began to die away. Grasses became the dominant plants across the Great Plains.

Grasslands dominated for millions of years before glaciation began. It is not clear why the Ice Age began, but the cold settled in. By twelve million years ago, ice had pushed its way to nearly where the Missouri and Mississippi Rivers now meet. As the glaciers retreated, they left behind plains of sand and silt. Strong winds spread this material over the Midwest. Land that emerged from directly under the ice sheets held rubble and gravel.

Iowa was glaciated over many thousands of years. As the glaciers repeatedly advanced and receded, they deposited particles of all sizes. The climate changed with ice and cold advancing and then retreating when the climate moderated. During warmer interglacial times, grasslands may have moved back into the Midwest from the south. Cornelia Mutel writes in *The Emerald Horizon* that fossil records of plants, small mammals, and snails show this migration of vegetation to and from south to north. As the climate moderated and the last glaciers melted, Iowa's plant communities began to resemble what we know today. Glaciers, their deposits, and water erosion created the landforms that shaped native prairies, woodlands, forests, and wetlands. These characteristics influenced how Euroamerican settlers later used the land.

As the climate warmed, it favored drought-tolerant grasslands, and they spread into the eastern edge of the Midwest. About fifty-five hundred years ago the grasslands moved across the Mississippi. This development was spurred by fire, a tool used today to manage prairies and woodlands. Lightning-ignited fire stimulated the growth of grasses. In the woods, fire stimulated fruit and nut production of trees and shrubs. Midwestern Native Americans set fires that burned the underbrush to open up the woodlands and increase visibility of approaching enemies. These burned areas also protected villages from fires caused by lightning strikes. The visions of these fires have contributed more remarkable prose from early settlers. Mutel includes in her book this quote from Thomas Macbride: "We saw the painted flames, like distant choppy waves on a sunrise-tinted sea."

The early settlers of the 1840s and 1850s practiced agriculture in a way unchanged in centuries, although they used iron and, then, steel plows. Their homesteads and towns did not have great impact on the natural landscape of prairies and woodlands. Small diversified farms maintained healthy soils. Small fields and mixed croplands and pastures left room for pockets of wildness. Mutel writes, "All human necessities were free for the taking. . . . The self-sufficient frontier landscape was short-lived." When the Industrial Revolution caught up with these farming families, they willingly and quickly changed their practices.

The Tractor and the Plow

The gas-powered tractor and the possibility of pulling a plow with machine power came in the early 1900s and altered the landscape forever. Prairie agriculture was revolutionized. New rail routes with their steam engines reached the Mississippi and beyond. The settlers soon came to rely on the railroad development and easily imported diverse supplies. The need to produce all commodities oneself disappeared once people could buy them in stores. Not only did the trains bring merchandise to the Midwest, but the midwestern farmers could send their agricultural products across the country. This led to more and more acres being developed for agricultural use. The greatest influx of settlers occurred in the late 1880s and early 1900s. They saw environmental costs as the necessary cost of development. Madson writes, "The old tallgrass prairie began to fade swiftly now." According to Savage, the wild prairie ecosystem was gone.

Farming expanded on the gently rolling and flatter land of the Midwest, leaving habitat for native plants and animals only on land less suited to agriculture. Today, some people driving through the Midwest may remark on the sameness of the terrain, but those who take the time to observe it more closely can imagine fields of prairie wildflowers and grasses. In Iowa the greatest amount of tallgrass prairie was destroyed. Intact prairie exists today on one-tenth of one percent of the state. Degradation of the soil through continuous farming and other development led to erosion and water pollution. With the decline of prairie habitat, the diversity and numbers of wildlife plummeted. Today remnant restorations of communities of native plants occur more successfully in woodlands because they were less disturbed than the prairies.

For over a hundred years, explorers, botanists, landscape architects and designers, and ecologists have recognized the value of the natural landscape and its swift degradation. How can it be that in the twenty-first century most people are unaware of and unconcerned about these changes? How was it possible that it took me so long to recognize our losses? When we buy and grow native plants, we start a discussion that needs to happen. As you will read in the following chapters, re-creating the lost landscape benefits everyone.

Wildlife

So far I have been discussing just one part of the native community, the plants. Missing parts are the insects, butterflies, birds and mammals, reptiles, and amphibians. These are as much a part of the prairie and woodlands as the grasses, wildflowers, trees, and shrubs. A thriving prairie has an amazing sound of buzzing bees as they and other insects surround the visitor who has come to see the flowers. She finds bees and butterflies, birds and toads. They are here because the plants provide food sources and locations to reproduce. The insects and butterflies pollinate the plants. Birds find insects to eat. Without viable, diverse communities such as these, we are losing species of wildlife rapidly.

3

Why Bring Native Plants into Our Gardens?

From the lay of the land—the flat expanses, rolling hills, ridges, and ravines—to the horizon line to the big sky, the midwestern landscape has a place in our residential landscapes. A gardener or landscape designer can learn to draw from the greater landscape when creating a garden rather than impose a design constructed without reference to the land. A specialty garden can be fun and even educational but seldom connects us to the place where we live. The native garden belongs here.

As a landscape designer, I found that reading the thoughts of other landscape designers, particularly those from the nineteenth and twentieth centuries, helped me to form this book. Robert Grese, editor of *The Native Landscape Reader*, wrote, "There is a long history of individuals who were urging greater attention to native flora and ecological processes and patterns in design." He continues: "Reconciling landscape design with the forms and patterns of nature is clearly one

4. A dragonfly feeds on selfheal (*Prunella vulgaris*). Photo by Deborah G. Groat.

of the central challenges of creating 'native gardens.'" Andrew Jackson Downing wrote that the greatest mistake is to study gardens too much and nature too little.

Jens Jensen wrote, in a 1920 essay titled "I Like Our Prairie Landscape," "Landscape gardening is the one art that is dependent upon the soil and climate conditions." He describes the Illinois landscape as "the garden of the prairie country."

Native gardens help us achieve sustainability. Perhaps overused, this term reminds us to think of the effect our home landscapes have on the larger environment. Without it we deplete fertility, create erosion, and often send poisoned water into waterways. By keeping water and organic matter on-site and using native plants that attract insects,

5. A soldier beetle is camouflaged on an oxeye false sunflower (*Heliopsis helianthoides*).

butterflies, mammals, and bees, we take steps to create an environment that is able to sustain itself (photo 4). As a Girl Scout I learned to
leave a site better than I found it. We returned it to its natural state by
removing traces of our stay and the stays of those who preceded us.
Jack Pizzo defines sustainability in the landscape context as capable of
being continued with minimal long-term impact.

According to Kim Eierman of EcoBeneficial, we should not just be
sustaining our landscapes but improving them. EcoBeneficial is a
horticulture communications and consulting company founded by
Eierman and dedicated to improving our environment by promoting
ecological landscaping and the use of native plants. She writes in her
blog and speaks to many audiences on the importance of diversity in

6. A male cardinal sits in an eastern redbud tree (*Cercis canadensis*) in spring. Photo by Deborah G. Groat.

the garden. She says that when you buy a house, you buy an ecosystem. You may be buying a future ecosystem or the promise of one. A healthy landscape provides ecosystem services. Every landscape matters. Every plant choice matters. When you choose to use native plants (many or a few), your garden becomes a natural fit to the space (photo 5).

Doug Tallamy explains the ecosystem services of insect species, including pollinating plants, returning nutrients tied up in dead plants and animals to the soil, keeping populations of insect herbivores in check, aerating and enriching the soil, and providing food directly or indirectly for most other animals. According to Tallamy and Rick Darke, "Stable ecosystems are more productive over the long term than unstable ones that fluctuate wildly in both species numbers and diversity." Native species are part of a greater network of relationships than nonnatives.

7. A red-winged blackbird lands on big bluestem (*Andropogon gerardii*) left standing from the previous year.

Including plants that serve as food and habitat for insects, butter-flies, birds, and mammals creates benefits for all occupants, includ-ing us. Watching butterflies and birds and seeing a succession of plant blooms draw us into the garden, the out-of-doors (photo 6). Eierman says, "We find the beauty in ecological function, not just in aesthetics." Wildlife appears that you would not have anticipated. She interviewed Doug Tallamy and wrote in her blog that his number-one native plant is the oak tree and number two is the cherry tree and related *Prunus* species. The volunteer cherry sapling that we so often remove from our landscapes provides sheltered habitat for numerous caterpillars, later filling our yards with butterflies and moths. This relationship between plants and butterflies is as beautiful as the butterflies themselves.

A large group of scientists, ecologists, and homeowners have found their life purpose in restoring the natural landscape. One of these

8. A spider's web hangs between Canada wild rye (*Elymus canadensis*) and goldenrod (*Solidago* species).

people, Connie Mutel, writes, "Restoration thus aims to reassemble our fractured native communities so they can once again function as diverse, self-sustaining units." From reading about these efforts and integrating native plants into my own landscape and my clients' landscapes, I have learned it is possible to create even small plant communities that bring diversity into the garden. For Pizzo environmental ecology means ensuring success in nature. Functional residential landscapes meeting homeowners' needs must also generate the ecosystem services required by diverse other species (photo 7).

Eierman describes the layered landscape, which most landscape designers understand. With large and small trees, shrubs, perennials, and grasses the gardener creates layers of habitat. Designers use

9. A honeybee feeds on a black-eyed Susan (*Rudbeckia hirta*), nearly blending in with the colors of the flower.

the layered landscape as a tool when designing with plants to create variety and beauty at all levels. The herbaceous layer (perennials and grasses) has the greatest potential botanical diversity. This greater diversity adds more color, form, fragrance, and texture to the garden. At the same time it provides more shelter and cover for wildlife (photo 8).

Eierman interviewed designer and horticulturalist C. Colston Burrell, who explained that a plant exists in an ecosystem, has an ecological niche, the appropriate context as part of the ecological community. The goals for a garden include, of course, beauty but also include that ecological community. Burrell makes the suggestion that we purposely leave the edges of our garden rough, not manicured, to create a bit more habitat. In addition he feels, and I agree, that we need to learn to accept a certain amount of damage to our plants, because when we kill the guilty bug, we are also killing many more (photo 9).

When I became a landscape designer in 1989, garden centers and wholesale nurseries offered a much smaller selection than they do in 2016. I chose plants from lists we learned in horticulture classes and plants that were available. Now, I no longer use some common nonnative plants because they have been found to invade natural areas. I came to use native plants when looking for replacements for invasive plants, including barberry (*Berberis* species), winged burning bush (*Euonymus alatus*), and vinca (*Vinca minor*). I learned that many of the plants filling nursery lots cause damage in natural areas. Their seeds travel by wind, bird, or mammal from the residential landscape to woodlands, roadsides, and railways where the seeds germinate, increasing the invasive plant population to the point of wiping out native species. These invasive nonnatives cannot support diverse wildlife. While designing gardens, I have referred hundreds of times to a book by Burrell, *Native Alternatives to Invasive Plants*, published by the Brooklyn Botanic Garden. He describes native plants we can substitute for invasive nonnatives. This publication gave me a wider understanding of how my work contributes to the protection of native species.

Nonnative plants and wildlife displace native species. We need to do more than plant natives. We need to refrain from planting species that invade. The natural pests of these exotics do not exist here to keep them in check. The exotics will grow faster and reproduce more successfully. They are not constrained by their natural enemies and are out of balance with their surrounding community. Making decisions about what to plant needs to take this into account. This is an argument for limiting the planting of exotics.

An author who has helped me understand diversity in the garden is entomologist Doug Tallamy. He writes that in parts of the United States there is no place left for wildlife but our gardens. His book, *Bringing Nature Home: How You Can Sustain Wildlife with Native Plants*, explains how plants and wildlife rely on each other. His was the first

10. A bumblebee busily travels between the flowers of wild bergamot (*Monarda fistulosa*) in a prairie.

book to explain how plants in our yards serve a diverse population of wildlife. The message is hopeful. Understanding plant communities will make our gardens supportive of a diverse environment. Gardeners play an important role by changing what food is available for their local wildlife (photo 10).

I learned in reading and rereading Tallamy's book that our native insects will not be able to survive on alien plant species. Our native birds need these native insects to survive. We can supply in our gardens the food and habitat birds and insects need. It can be as simple as that.

I described earlier how agriculture and other development filled the Midwest. As a result of these changes, native plant communities became smaller and smaller islands. These spaces are too small to prevent the local or total extinction of many species. Tallamy says we can coexist with these species if we understand their and our needs for a healthy environment. "We remove species from our nation's ecosystems at the risk of their complete collapse." He writes, "It is not only possible but highly desirable from a human perspective to create living spaces that are themselves functioning, sustainable ecosystems with high species diversity." Many agree with him that biodiversity is a national treasure.

One example given in his book is the monarch butterfly. A popular plant in North America is the butterfly bush (*Buddleia* species), which attracts butterflies with its nectar. It is not fully hardy in the Midwest and often dies back during the winter, so it is not a great landscape plant. In the warmer hardiness zones of the Midwest, this plant survives the winter and can invade natural areas. The caterpillar produced by the butterfly from the eggs deposited on the plant cannot eat the leaves of this plant. They are not a food source for the caterpillar, so it dies and does not become a butterfly. The native milkweed (*Asclepias* species) supports the life cycle of the monarch butterfly. I most often plant butterfly weed (*A. tuberosa*) for its showy orange flowers and also use swamp milkweed (*A. incarnata*) with its pink flower in my prairie designs. This plant, despite its name, is not a weed. Our landscapes need to be places where animals and plants can successfully reproduce. According to Darke and Tallamy, our residential landscapes become a public resource.

Reading words written in the early 1900s about plant ecology and plant associations, I wonder how we have managed to do so much damage to our plant communities in a century. The effects have been called out frequently in the past three or four decades, but these people were not heard sufficiently. Now armed with closer observations and investigations, we have information and processes to follow to begin to rectify the damage.

Elsa Rehmann in her 1933 essay "An Ecological Approach" writes that plant ecology influences landscape design. A plant is no longer native if it is transferred to a locality in which it is not really indigenous. She worries about the increasing need to wipe out whole sections of native growth by "suburban colonies" where owners have come to the country to live. She describes restoration efforts where the native vegetation can reestablish itself. A footnote to this essay by the editor of the collection, Robert Grese, adds that the word "ecology" dates back to 1866.

Aldo Leopold in his 1926 essay, "The Last Stand of the Wilderness," wrote, "How many of those whole-hearted conservationists who berate the past generation for its short-sightedness in the use of natural resources have stopped to ask themselves for what new evils the next generation will berate us?" He continues: "When the end of the supply is in sight we 'discover' that the thing is valuable." Leopold's words have been a call to action for many.

Leopold wrote that the wilderness is close to exhaustion. The supply of natural resources always seemed unlimited, but now the end is in sight. The first settlers in Dane County, Wisconsin, found soil, flora, and fauna in perfect balance. Agriculture and industry developed until they had sapped the soil of its fertility. "In geological reckoning of time, things happened with the suddenness of catastrophes," Paul Riis wrote in 1937 in an essay about the efforts of the Ecological Garden and Arboretum at the University of Wisconsin to protect and restore eight hundred acres of land that had been degraded. These events took place across the Midwest.

Robert Grese, in his epilogue to *The Native Landscape Reader*, writes of the value of native gardens for wildlife. He believes as I do that if homeowners across the country added wildlife habitat to a portion of their yard, a connection can develop between them and county, state, and national parks and natural areas. Fortunately, there is a growing interest in native gardens and ecological restoration.

Planning the Garden

We make efforts to plan nearly every aspect of our lives. It should come as no surprise that our gardens need planning also. Once I had a conversation with a naturalist, a person who made his living constructing and maintaining large native areas. He did not understand what I did, assuming it was unconnected to his line of work. I explained that what we do is very similar. We make thoughtful plans and implement them, creating spaces for people to be outside.

What Is Garden or Landscape Design?

Landscape design is a hidden art. Although I have been a voracious reader since I was a child and have visited numerous museums and parks, I was not aware of landscape design and the designer until I was in my early thirties. This seems very strange since gardens have been settings for hundreds of novels and movies and subjects for thousands of paintings. It was through my love of gardening, and daylilies in particular, that I became aware of the profession of landscape design. The profession does not have visibility even as it is everywhere. So it is not surprising that few homeowners have utilized garden design. I find that many people do not understand what it is or feel it is beyond their realm because they think it costs too much or focuses too much on what you can or cannot do in your landscape.

The word "garden" describes the place where we sit, think, dream, play, cook, swim, and grow things. Sometimes it is private; sometimes, public. It is a family space into which we invite friends and neighbors. Humans have created gardens for centuries. They provided relief from the sun, a place to grow food, a place to meet, a private place, and a place of beauty. Our gardens envelop our homes and bring out their best features. Sometimes we want the entry to welcome visitors with open arms, and other times we build boundaries for privacy or to create a sense of mystery. In this chapter you will see some examples.

Landscape designers use elements basic to all kinds of design. They use scale to show relationships of objects to each other and make people comfortable in a garden. They use balance for the same reason and also to create beauty. They will repeat plants or other objects to lead visitors' eyes in a particular direction. Designers choose plants and materials whose forms (shapes), textures (variety), colors, and lines create these effects. It is not by chance that we enjoy spending time in a well-designed garden.

The word "design" means to plan with intent, to create meaningful, useful, and beautiful spaces. Making a plan for whatever activity we attempt is a recipe for success. It does not mean we cannot ever be impulsive or surprised. It just means that we are more likely to get it right and to be pleased with our results. John Brookes, a well-known and thoughtful English designer, writes, "You wouldn't dream of introducing a new baby to a household without making any nursery preparations, and it's the same with plants: both are living things, and both need nurseries." An advantage of having a plan is in the implementation. A plan makes it easy to divide the construction into affordable phases that make sense and will eliminate costly do-overs.

Before making a plan, we make lists and ask ourselves questions. When I meet with clients, I have many questions because I want the design to work for them. While studying landscape design, I began to develop a sheet of questions I would ask every client. By the time I started working, I had a thorough list. I wrote it out on a sheet of paper and put the sheet in a transparent sleeve. I slipped it into my briefcase and still have it today. Over time, I felt less need to refer to it as the questions became second nature to me. As our world and climate change, I add new questions about water use, the time people have for gardening, and their concerns about the environment.

No two gardens are the same; they are individualized to the people living there. Every site has inherent problems such as poor soils, steep grades, small side yards, close neighbors, erosion-prone soils, or too much or too little sun. It is the job of the designer to mitigate these problems and incorporate the desires of the client. The goal is to make a garden that the homeowners will enjoy.

As I learn more about native plants, prairies, savannas, and woodlands, I try to incorporate parts of the natural landscape into my yard first and then into my clients'. I always feel more confident adding a plant to a client's plan when I have grown it previously in my own yard. In doing so, I find an amazing variety of plants to use and become even more aware of the benefits of using them. The beauty, interest, and habitat in these gardens convinced me to pursue the use of these plants.

I began on a small scale, turning two approximately eight- by twelve-foot gardens I had previously used for vegetables into native gardens. I studied information and catalogs picked up at workshops or fairs. I read the first books I had bought about prairies. I ordered plugs from the Ion Exchange in Harpers Ferry, Iowa. The plants arrived, and they were tiny with very little tops and small balls of roots. I wondered if they were viable. I had made a plan using color and height to decide how to place the plugs in groups of each variety. I planted the plugs and carefully mulched around them. Most of them survived, growing into my first prairie gardens.

My husband developed an interest in the prairie landscape, and after reading through my library, he planted his first large prairie area. Since then he has added two more with paths that we, our visitors, and our two dogs use to see the prairie up close.

I began to add native plants to my ornamental gardens. They provided a way to increase the variety of plants and create new combinations. The grasses appealed to me, and I planted switch grass (*Panicum* species), little bluestem (*Schizachyrium scoparium*), northern sea oats (*Chasmanthium latifolium*), and tufted hair grass (*Deschampsia cespitosa*). I had varying amounts of success but now know better ways to incorporate them in gardens. I had developed a love of ornamental grasses, using them in my and clients' gardens. Now, however, I stay with native grasses as they have become readily available. The one nonnative grass I continue to use is Karl Foerster feather reed grass (*Calamagrostis* × *acutiflora* 'Karl Foerster') because I have not seen it appear where it has not been planted.

Writing this book has shown me that I need to do more to incorporate native plants in gardens and that I have been missing opportunities to do so. I am excited to continue to garden and design gardens. In the past few years, clients have come to me seeking a design that incorporates native plants and brings wildlife to their yards. I feel there is a great interest in these plants, and I worry that if they are used without adequate planning, people will give up on them or have unsuccessful experiences. Every gardener has had a failure of some kind and learns from it. However, it is much more pleasant to have success from the start. A well-planned garden will mean fewer false starts.

Planning the Garden

As you begin to plan your garden, the most important part is to know the property well. Observe it in all seasons. Notice how the sun moves overhead and how the wind moves through. Where will the snow drift? John Brookes writes that climate dictates the interaction of the house with the garden. What are the contours? What kind of soil exists on the site? Are there high or low spots? How does the yard look from the street? What are the views from inside the house? What path do you take when walking about the yard? Do you need an area of lawn for sunbathing or play? Would you like to screen your neighbors' deck or open a view into their landscape? Do you need a play area for children? Would you like to attract and feed birds?

List the activities you will undertake in the yard: entertaining, vegetable gardening, meditating, cooking. Write down your favorite plants and colors. Is there a need to redirect rainwater? Ask yourself if you really enjoy working in the garden, or do you need a low-maintenance garden? All gardens will need some maintenance, even native gardens. Also note where utilities and easements exist. Are there adequate water sources? Do you need tool storage? What is your budget?

Plants make up only a portion of garden design. Paths, landings, patios, decks, fire pits, ponds, swimming pools, pergolas, arbors, sheds, play structures, and outdoor kitchens offer endless possibilities. With a list of questions and answers and a budget, the gardener chooses which elements will work in the landscape.

Often, after we have walked around their yard and made some lists, clients will ask me what my ideas are. I tell them I need to put the site down on paper (or the computer screen). I need to consider every bit of information, incorporate everything I have seen and heard, and even research additional sources before I formulate a presentable plan. I need to create a site plan to see all parts in relation to each other. There are dynamics at play that become evident only at this point. It is like a chess game where every move affects the outcome.

So I encourage gardeners to get it down on paper to avoid unpleasant surprises. The drawing does not have to be fancy. It just has to include the information you have gathered. Graph paper helps. And draw in pencil.

Before starting your exploration of the dimensions of your yard, try to find existing plans. A previous owner may have had a plan drawn. Your property's abstract may have a site plan that shows property lines, easements, and the location of your house. Your city or county recorder's or assessor's office usually has the same information. Ask for subdivision plans. Very often these are available online on the county assessor's website. Knowing the location of your property lines will prevent future disagreements with neighbors.

With your clipboard, paper, pencil, and tape measure, record the location of all existing elements on your site. This includes the house, windows, porch, walk, driveway, fence, shed, utility boxes and lines, downspouts, trees and shrubs, garden areas, and anything else you see. Measure as accurately as possible. The result may look like a secret code, but after you go inside and decipher your marks and record them on a clean sheet of paper, you will have a solid beginning for your plan. Garden design software for the homeowner is available if you are interested.

One more indispensable tool is the camera. Since most mobile phones now include cameras, photographing your yard is easy. Take a series of photographs of the front of the house from the street. Take another of the yard from the front of the house. Consider the views from inside the house, out the windows. Record all elements—how the walk meets the house, how the driveway meets the street. Take photos from the end of each property line to define the boundaries of the yard. Photograph every plant and all hard elements like patios and decks. Download the photos to a computer and start to plan.

The drawing you are making is the plan or bird's-eye view. It will not show elevations, but the photographs you take will add that information in pictures. Drawing on tracing paper laid over a photograph will give you an idea of how certain plants will look in your yard. Draw in the plants and other elements you plan to use as you would see them while standing in the yard.

I create a design statement or purpose to share with my client and to keep me on track. I develop the statement or purpose after reviewing all the information gathered from talking to the homeowners and walking and photographing the site. It reminds me of the goal during the entire design process. The idea is to write down what you would like to accomplish and its major parts in the form of a list or a diagram.

A recent project can serve as an example. A couple, recent retirees, love their home and neighborhood but enjoy traveling. While away, they do not want to worry about their yard and do not want to have a lot of yard work waiting for them when they return. They enjoy being in the yard, and a moderate amount of maintenance is manageable. They have a water problem in the front yard, and even though they have spent money on tiling and lawn repair, the problem persists. They decided it is time to have a redesign for the front yard that solves the water problem.

This description was the basis for my design statement, which included solving the water problem by creating an area where water can collect during heavy rains before entering the ground. This helps prevent erosion of the lawn. We solved the difficulty of growing lawn grass in the shade by designing a garden of low-maintenance native and nonnative plants. We brightened the area by adding native limestone stepping-stones and outcropping stone. All of this needed to be accomplished while protecting two large shade trees. Writing down goals will direct your energy toward real solutions.

Once you complete a site plan, the more enjoyable part of designing the garden begins. On tracing paper placed over the site plan, draw circles to show the different use areas. Check out the best locations for seating, a vegetable garden, a prairie garden, or a cutting garden. Draw in screening where it is needed. Consider each element you have listed on your checklist. This process gives you the opportunity to experiment with placement of activity areas and beds. You will be able to see the connections between them. Is it comfortable? Is there room to move your wheelbarrow? Is there access to the water hydrant or spigot? Will your plants receive adequate sun or shade? Is there a place to sit and view the garden?

Many accomplished designers and teachers have written excellent books on garden design, which I have listed in the resources section. They include sample checklists, supply lists, illustrations of site and concept plans, and photographs of gardens. These books will take you through the design process step by step. In this book, I have applied my knowledge of landscape design to designing with native plants. The key is to know the size, habit, and needs of native plants, just as with any plant. Acknowledging the more "wild" or "natural" look of native plants will help you decide how best to use them in your garden. Challenges you may face include finding an adequate selection of plants from which to choose, finding a particular plant you want to buy, and finding knowledgeable sales help in garden centers.

Vanessa Nagel explains in *Understanding Garden Design* that planning precedes design. It provides the basis to make decisions during the design process. She writes, "When we apply a skillful process of design to a garden, there will likely be greater agreement that the garden is beautiful."

I can imagine that some readers will not take on a landscape redesign but simply want to plant. I appreciate that you have stuck with me this far, giving my argument for planning a chance. As a plant lover and gardener I understand. I have gone to the garden center with one or two plants in mind and come home with a carful. I have designed on the fly, thinking, "Oh, I can move that later." But when you use a new palette of native plants, extra planning will pay off. Do try to take the time to make lists and ask yourself questions before going shopping. Assess your conditions. Read about plant requirements and possible combinations. According to John Brookes, "Design is to do with logic and suitability and, increasingly, sustainability."

As mentioned earlier, the gardener often begins to use native plants by adding them to an existing landscape. These plants complement each other and thrive if they require similar conditions. Many wonderful gardens combine both native and nonnative plants. Some nonnative plants such as peonies, lilacs, Russian sage, and catmint provide deer resistance, an important asset in the Midwest. The gardens described in this chapter provide examples of combining these plants. These gardens have been created on large and small scales, and the design elements exist in most landscapes.

11. Native trees swamp white oak (*Quercus bicolor*) and serviceberry (*Amelanchier canadensis*) create a natural scene with the shrub coralberry (*Symphoricarpos orbiculatus*) and grasses Shenandoah switch grass (*Panicum virgatum* 'Shenandoah') and side oats grama (*Bouteloua curtipendula*). Photo by Jason Allen.

Entry Gardens

Often I am asked to redesign the area around a front door, to create an entry garden. Many times the entry garden is the first part of a landscape design that is installed. This area welcomes visitors and creates a presence that causes people to look twice as they walk or drive by. Sometimes it includes adding a porch, deck, patio, pergola, or steps. The entry garden is a perfect place to highlight native plants.

A garden designed by Jason Allen of Country Landscapes covers the large entry area of a home in Iowa. It spans a curved driveway and generous-sized cobble paver walk. Using shrubs, grasses, and trees, Allen created a natural, peaceful welcome to this home. Shrubs and trees give a landscape structure year-round, something using only grasses and wildflowers does not achieve, although they can provide textural interest in the winter. The design invites the visitor to enjoy the walk up to the front door. The trees used are swamp white oak

(*Quercus bicolor*) and serviceberry (*Amelanchier canadensis*). The use of stone as it might occur in nature adds to the sense of place this garden evokes (photo 11).

The next example also shows an entry to a large home but with a less restrained and less sculptural design than the previous example, where each element was distinct. These different design styles may arise from house architecture, setting, client preferences, and designer ideas and are usually a combination of all of them. Here the plants work together to create a naturalistic effect, although a mixture of native and nonnative plants. Much naturalistic planting today is done with native and nonnative plants, such as the work of Piet Oudolf in the Lurie Garden in Chicago and the High Line Garden in New York City. A taller and wilder combination of plants along the driveway transitions to shorter plants in front of the house. The journey to the home is exciting, and the arrival is welcoming. Salsbury-Schweyer, Inc., designed and installed this project in Ohio (photo 12).

Out the Back Door

Endless possibilities for backyard garden design exist. Many of these create opportunities to use native plants, whether the overall plan is naturalistic or traditional. Even a new home on a traditional lot improves with the addition of beautiful native flowering plants. Try adding a few native plants to your garden beds, but consider this only a beginning to increasing the role of native plants in the landscape.

I was asked by a couple with a great interest in the Iowa prairie to design their landscape. Their greatest concern was a need for screening from their close neighbors. They had built a new house on a corner lot in a new subdivision, and the neighborhood rapidly filled with new homes and barren yards. Their yard included views of three separate utility boxes and surrounding houses and, fortunately, a clump of native trees, eastern cottonwood (*Populus deltoides*). Using mostly native plants, I created screens of the utility boxes, neighbors, and streets. The design encloses small areas of lawn with beds of native plants. For instant screening and structure, I used Black Hills spruce

12. Purple coneflower (*Echinacea purpurea*), yarrow (*Achillea* species), and catmint (*Nepeta* species) create views for visitors as well as for those in the house. Photo by Salsbury-Schweyer, Inc.

(*Picea glauca densata*), Iseli Foxtail spruce (*P. pungens* 'Iseli Foxtail'), Rainbow Pillar shadblow serviceberry (*Amelanchier canadensis* 'Rainbow Pillar'), and the existing trees. I filled the beds with shrubs and grasses and perennials, using flats or plugs whenever possible. These vigorous, small nursery plants adapt quickly in landscapes.

A continuous bed curves around the backyard. On one end, the existing trees support a small shade garden. On the other end, the bed curves around the corner to screen utility boxes, neighbors, and the street. Even though the screen is not solid, it provides privacy and creates a lovely backyard space. The shrubs used include Autumn Jazz viburnum (*Viburnum dentatum* 'Autumn Jazz'), bottlebrush buckeye (*Aesculus parviflora*), Gro-Low fragrant sumac (*Rhus aromatica* 'Gro-Low'), and Summer Wine ninebark (*Physocarpus opulifolia* 'Seward'). The viburnum, sumac, and ninebark used are cultivars and more compact than the species and work well in residential landscapes. The shrubs provide color and interest spring, summer, and fall with leaf and flower color and structure in the winter. They are also habitat and food sources for birds and insects.

13. This bed wraps around a corner of the yard and provides screening with a combination of Black Hills spruce (*Picea glauca densata*) and native perennials and grasses, including prairie blazing star (*Liatris pycnostachya*), copper-shouldered oval sedge (*Carex bicknellii*), and prairie dropseed (*Sporobolus heterolepis*).

14. Another corner screens the neighbors' backyards with Iseli Foxtail spruce (*Picea pungens* 'Iseli Foxtail') and Rainbow Pillar shadblow serviceberry (*Amelanchier canadensis* 'Rainbow Pillar').

15. Seen from the rear property line, the backyard is nicely screened by gray-headed coneflower (*Ratibida pinnata*), Indian grass (*Sorghastrum nutans*), prairie blazing star (*Liatris pycnostachya*), and big bluestem (*Andropogon gerardii*).

Perennials include false blue indigo (*Baptisia australis*), big bluestem (*Andropogon gerardii*), prairie blazing star (*Liatris pycnostachya*), pale purple coneflower (*Echinacea pallida*), Goldsturm black-eyed Susan (*Rudbeckia fulgida* 'Goldsturm'), Walker's Low catmint (*Nepeta racemosa* 'Walker's Low'), Kit Kat catmint (*N.* × *faassenii* 'Kit Kat'), May Night salvia (*Salvia nemorosa* 'Mainacht'), Indian grass (*Sorghastrum nutans*), gray-headed coneflower (*Ratibida pinnata*), and little bluestem (*Schizachyrium scoparium*). The flowers bloom from spring through fall, and the grasses fill out the garden year-round (photos 13–15).

Where Does All the Water Go?

When I begin to assess a site, the first thing I ask is, "Where is all the rainwater going?" The best answer is that it stays on-site, that the ground within the property absorbs all of it. The benefits include holding moisture for the landscape plants; no erosion of the topsoil; beds that do not wash out during rainfall events; mulch that stays in place; less water entering the sewer system, lakes, streams, and rivers; and cleaner water that filters through the soil before entering groundwater stores.

On most lots, the downspouts are the greatest source of water that adversely affects the landscape. During rainfall water gushes out and spills onto beds, lawns, driveways, and walks. Water that runs over driveways or off the street contains pollutants that degrade our water sources. Gas, oil, salt, fertilizers, and pesticides move with the water. Water that cannot be absorbed by beds erodes soil and moves mulch. Sometimes it enters our or our neighbors' basements. I look at the gutters and the roof line to learn which parts of the roof are shedding the most water. Can some of it be diverted to a different or additional downspout? How can I direct the water within the landscape?

I know that this does not sound like a glamorous or an exciting place to start designing the most beautiful native garden in the neighborhood. However, this kind of observation often leads to a wonderfully creative solution. Sometimes it will be a simple change of redirecting the downspout or burying it so that it surfaces away from the house or empties into a buried drain. Adding a rain garden to the yard can help keep water on-site and at the same time create a beautiful garden.

Low areas in your yard that collect water are not suitable locations for rain gardens. For a rain garden to serve its purpose, which is to collect water and allow it to absorb into the ground, it must be an area that drains well. The circumstances in your yard may not allow a rain garden. They need to be at least ten feet from the house because you do not want to add water to the ground near the house. The area needs to be free of utilities to accommodate digging a basin. The bottom of the rain garden needs to be level. If the ground slopes, you will need to build a wall on one end to create a level bottom. You will need at least a partly sunny location.

In the appropriate location, rain gardens are a great opportunity to use native plants. One example of a favorable location is where a downspout empties, as long as you direct the water at least ten feet away from the house. Another would be an area of the lawn that receives water running off a driveway. The roots of mature native plants reach deeply into the ground, enabling the plants to use water far below the surface. When a rain garden dries out, which will happen between rains, the plants need to survive. Plants that can tolerate standing water are planted in the center of the rain garden, while those that like well-drained soil are planted on the sloping sides. Rainscaping Iowa provides instruction and information on constructing rain gardens. There are other sources of information as well in the resources list.

When a rain garden is not feasible, I often use some of the same principles I used for a home in Iowa City (photos 16–17). The downspout at the corner of the house emptied into a drain that dispersed the water onto the lawn. We took advantage of the drain and let the slope of the yard cause the water to enter a bed. We placed a few cobbles in the bed to slow the movement of the water and prepared the bed with added compost to help retain the water and encourage absorption. The area is very narrow and between the edge of the driveway and the neighbor's yard. We created a small berm on the neighbor's side. Util-

16. A drain in the lawn empties above a bed of native plants. Cobbles slow the movement of water into the bed so that the soil and mulch do not wash out onto the driveway and sidewalk.

17. A buried tile line from the house empties just below the wall onto cobbles, which slow the movement of the water and allow it to enter the ground.

ity lines run below the garden to the house. Native prairie plants fill the garden and attract beneficial caterpillars and subsequently butterflies. On the other side of the driveway, we planted another garden to catch rainwater from the house before it reaches the street. The plants, which were four-inch plugs, include butterfly weed (*Asclepias tuberosa*), smooth blue aster (*Symphyotrichum ericoides*), brown fox sedge (*Carex vulpinoidea*), prairie blazing star (*Liatris pycnostachya*), black-eyed Susan (*Rudbeckia hirta*), little bluestem (*Schizachyrium scoparium*), and prairie dropseed (*Sporobolus heterolepis*).

I designed a project in Coralville, Iowa, with two rain gardens that replaced most of the front lawn of the lot (photos 18–20). The yard

18. On the side of the upper rain garden, limestone steps lead from a path at the top of the garden. Additional pieces of limestone slow water that overflows during heavy rains.

19. From butterfly weed (*Asclepias tuberosa*) to Culver's root (*Veronicastrum virginicum*), these rain gardens glow with native plants.

20. During heavy rains, the rain gardens performed beautifully. Photo by Margaret Kiekhaefer.

sloped downward toward the street, so we installed a wall to level the bottom of the lower rain garden. Overflow from the top garden enters the lower garden. Runoff from the driveway also enters the lower garden. This area includes two existing trees, so we used shade-tolerant plants in the lower garden. The year we installed this landscape, heavy rain occurred multiple times and the gardens handled the water well. We made a few adjustments to the overflow areas so that the mulch and soil would not be displaced.

We began the project by building a wall to support the front yard along the house foundation where the slope was eroding. Once that was complete, we constructed the two basins. At the top of the first basin, a path leads to steps down the side of the rain garden. Along the edge of the upper basin, we added an overflow area with pieces of limestone to slow the water flow.

The homeowner wanted native plants, and we chose a variety for the garden. The plants include prairie dropseed (*Sporobolus heterolepis*), butterfly weed (*Asclepias tuberosa*), swamp milkweed (*A. incarnata*), wild blue indigo (*Baptisia australis*), spotted Joe Pye weed (*Eupatorium maculatum*), prairie blazing star (*Liatris pycnostachya*), spiked gayfeather (*L. spicata*), black-eyed Susan (*Rudbeckia hirta*), Culver's root (*Veronicastrum virginicum*), common spiderwort (*Tradescantia ohiensis*), and golden alexanders (*Zizia aurea*). These plants tolerate both dry and wet soil so adapt well to the conditions of a rain garden, and we placed them accordingly. I know this is a long list, but I want to show the variety of native plants available to gardeners.

Plants preferring well-drained soil were planted along the edges and sides of the garden, while those that tolerate wet soils were planted in the center. Many of these plants attract butterflies. We also used some nonnative plants: lady's mantle (*Alchemilla mollis*), coral bells (*Heuchera* species), catmint (*Nepeta* species), and yarrow (*Achillea* species). Lady's mantle and coral bells look best when planted in areas of afternoon shade, while catmint and yarrow thrive in sun. The photos show the garden in summer and in fall after heavy rains.

We travel to Minnesota to look at the next garden designed, installed, maintained, and photographed by EnergyScapes (photo 21). This rain garden resulted from water problems in both homes where downspouts flowed into the narrow side yard. The solution included a swale to quickly drain the excess water toward the street but slow it down once it was far enough from those foundations. The swale is filled with common spiderwort (*Tradescantia ohiensis*), prairie dropseed (*Sporobolus heterolepis*), and No Mow Lawn Seed Mix of fine fescues from Prairie Nursery. The brown area in the center of the No Mow is a ridge designed to slow flow and create a rain garden above that point, twenty feet from each home.

21. Neighbors share a rain garden that takes and absorbs rainwater from both lots. Photo by Douglas Owens-Pike.

Paths

After looking at water movement, I consider pedestrian movement or circulation around the yard. I draw lines or arrows on my plan to experiment with possible routes. Where does the homeowner need to walk to get to a shed or the patio? Is there a way to get the wheelbarrow from the garage to the backyard? Do visitors know where to park and approach the house? What is the best way to walk through the garden or have access for gardening chores? Some of these activities require paths.

One of the goals of a landscape designer is to bring homeowners or guests outside and into the landscape. Paths serve as a great tool to connect people with nature. This may seem obvious, but if you drive around your town, I bet you will see that most homes have no clear connection to the yard. Instead we create barriers of foundation plantings and narrow, uncomfortable walks and front stoops or porches.

Paths provide a perfect location for a combination of low- to medium-height native wildflowers and grasses. They indicate the edge of the path and help direct pedestrians where you would like them to go: the mailbox, the garage, the street, the backyard, through a gate, or to a special secret garden. Materials vary from grass and stepping-stones to pavers and river rock or pea gravel. Sometimes the path will traverse a grade, so steps are needed. Dense plantings of natives along the steps will create a pleasing barrier that indicates the edge of the steps.

In an Iowa project designed by Jason Allen, a path made of large rectangular stones leads to the front door, clearly showing visitors how to approach the entry. They pass by a rich, low, peaceful, and inviting planting

22. A planting of native and nonnative perennials, grasses, and shrubs provides a low enclosure for a porch and welcomes visitors to walk along the path. Photo by Jason Allen.

23. The use of native stone steps and plants created access to the backyard of this home, where previously there had been a dark area, thick with weeds.

of grasses and perennials that complements the house and does not completely obscure the long ground-level porch. Allen used Russian sage (*Perovskia atriplicifolia*), prairie dropseed (*Sporobolus heterolepis*), little bluestem (*Schizachyrium scoparium*), catmint (*Nepeta* species), Karl Foerster feather reed grass (*Calamagrostis × acutiflora* 'Karl Foerster') Shenandoah switch grass (*Panicum virgatum* 'Shenandoah'), and Sunrise Sunset rose (*Rosa* 'Sunrise Sunset'), all deer resistant except the rose (photo 22).

Local native stone contributes a sense of longevity to a project. As soon as the stone is installed, it appears to have always been there. In this next Iowa project with a very narrow, steep, and shady side yard, limestone supplied a solution. The steps and path provided access to the backyard, blended well with the neighbor's landscape, and lightened up the area. Prior to the landscaping, the area was not accessible. Existing hosta and arborvitae now join native ferns, perennials,

24. The native limestone steps provide a safe path to the front yard.

and shrubs. The plants include cinnamon fern (*Osmunda cinnamomea*), Allegheny foamflower (*Tiarella cordifolia*), black snakeroot (*Cimicifuga racemosa*), Carolina allspice (*Calycanthus floridus*), and vernal witch hazel (*Hamamelis vernalis*). Carolina allspice is a large, deer-resistant shrub that grows in sun or shade. Vernal witch hazel has a yellow-red flower that blooms in very early spring before its leaves emerge. This home borders a natural area, and using native perennials, shrubs, and small trees in the landscape connects the garden to its surroundings (photos 23–24).

Beds and Borders

Who does not want a beautiful perennial bed or border? Magazines and books are full of them. They stretch around houses and through yards. Gorgeous colors the range of a rainbow flow into each other from spring to fall. And then there is winter interest as well. I have two

25. Choosing plants with different flower and leaf shapes, in addition to different colors and heights, makes a garden interesting.

questions. How can we lessen the maintenance of these gardens, and how can we bring ecological diversity to them? I certainly do not want to rip out my large border, but I can begin to replace plants that I have learned are invasive nonnatives or plants that are not holding their own. When beginning a new bed, I can have a fresh start. This means paying attention to soil and exposure needs of native plants. I can still choose plants for their size, their bloom time, and year-round interest. Native plants will not need soil as rich or fertile as we have been used to preparing. Well-draining soil, however, remains important.

In my gardens at home, I have created numerous combinations of plants using natives and in the process learned more about them. Many will weave their way gracefully through a bed. Others assert their presence. Some just do not make suitable companions. An early successful attempt to incorporate native plants into a perennial bed in my front yard (photo 25) includes blazing star (*Liatris spicata*), queen of the prairie (*Filipendula rubra* 'Venusta Magnifica'), Goldsturm black-eyed Susan (*Rudbeckia fulgida* 'Goldsturm'), fernleaf yarrow (*Achillea filipendulina*), and a daylily in midsummer. They serve as respectful companions to the rest of the garden, although the black-eyed Susan sometimes dominates. Somehow, when plants intermingle, we feel great pleasure. It is something that can be hard to plan, but over time we learn which plants make good companions.

Ponds

Everyone loves a pond. We are drawn to them. On the many garden tours I have attended, a pond will attract visitors immediately. Whether it is the sound of the water, the reflection of the sky, the surroundings, or comfortable seating, this never fails to happen.

Every garden does not need a pond, and the building costs and maintenance need to be considered as well as safety. But the possibilities for pond design are endless. A pond and its plantings attract more birds and insects to the garden. However, most ponds or other water features I see in midwestern gardens, although they may be beauti-

26. Creating a pond with such a natural appearance requires long study of nature. Photo by Jack Pizzo.

fully constructed, look out of place in the landscape. I have thought of building a pond to remind us of the sinkholes that existed across the prairie and now have nearly disappeared as farmers have tiled the land for their row crops. These sinkholes provided habitat for waterfowl through the seasons.

An example from Pizzo Associates shows a pond on a small estate near Chicago. The landscape was restored following an original Jens Jensen planting plan, using blue flag iris (*Iris virginica* var. *shrevei*), sedges (*Carex* species), and native hibiscus (*Hibiscus* species). The artful design creates a setting one might come across while hiking through woods (photo 26).

Foundation Plantings

Landscape designers tend to hold foundation plantings in low regard. We all have seen house after house and street after street of poorly trimmed yews and junipers that have outgrown their allotted space and probably should not have been planted in the first place. The poured-concrete foundations of today's homes call out for coverage. When planting around a house, I like to make wide beds with room enough for layers of plants. Shrubs and perennials and even a small tree add beauty and comfort.

Gardeners and designers have planted imaginative foundation plantings composed of native plants. These plants have the capacity to soften hard edges, screen unsightly concrete and utility boxes, and create beautiful spaces. What better place to start introducing native plants into your yard than the beds around the house. Begin with a side or back of the house if you are unsure of the outcome.

Debbie Groat transformed her Illinois landscape using native plants, and her projects are wonderful examples of what is possible. She designed and planted a lovely shade garden on the side of her house. A small native tree and perennials fill this curved bed and present a cool, peaceful view. Plants include pagoda dogwood (*Cornus alternifolia*), wild geranium (*Geranium maculatum*), Solomon's seal (*Polygonatum* species), and wild ginger (*Asarum canadense*) (photo 27). The pagoda dogwood is one of my favorite plants. The horizontal branching gives the tree its common name. This dogwood prefers partial shade, blooms white in the spring, produces a dark blue berry, and has maroon fall leaf color. It grows slowly, and finding large specimens in the garden center is rare.

On the sunny side of the house, Groat planted a bed that starts near the front door and follows the entire front side of the house. Again she has used perennials and a tree but also shrubs. Here the plants screen the house and soften its rectangular shape. Plants include prairie smoke (*Geum triflorum*), common spiderwort (*Tradescantia ohiensis*), obedient plant (*Physostegia virginiana*), butterfly weed (*Asclepias*

27. A pagoda dogwood (*Cornus alternifolia*), a native ornamental tree, brightens the garden in spring. The tree is underplanted with native perennials that thrive in shade. Photo by Deborah G. Groat.

28. Short to tall summer-blooming, native wildflowers welcome visitors. Photo by Deborah G. Groat.

tuberosa), black-eyed Susan (*Rudbeckia hirta*), wild bergamot (*Monarda fistulosa*), and pale purple coneflower (*Echinacea pallida*). Groat planted this garden in front of a traditional evergreen hedge that the garden completely obscures from view (photo 28). This landscape gives visitors a wonderful taste of native gardening.

Built Landscape

Built landscape refers to hardscaping or any nonplant or soil (such as a berm) element of the garden. Commonly this includes walls, walks, patios, fencing, arbors, and pergolas. The materials include stone, wood, poured concrete, brick and concrete pavers, and con-

29. In a residential neighborhood, a well-planned backyard provides a native refuge for birds, insects, and people. Photo by Salsbury-Schweyer, Inc.

crete blocks. Designers use repurposed materials as well as glass and Plexiglas. From the garden designer's point of view, the garden is not complete until plants have been added, hopefully planned from the beginning of the process so they do not look as though someone has just dropped them in as an afterthought. I see many photographs in magazines and catalogs showing finished hardscapes with only spots of green here or there.

The plants garden designers choose give the site life. Without them the landscape is incomplete, not comfortably habitable by humans or wildlife. Using stone or other materials in the landscape presents an opportunity to create a garden. When we sit outside, we like to surround ourselves with the color and texture of plants. Use native plants

30. Many different landscape materials complement native plants, including native limestone and cast concrete in natural color tones.

in these settings. They blend wonderfully with native stone and can soften the hard edges of concrete pavers and stones.

Salsbury-Schweyer, Inc., designed and built a beautiful seating area surrounded by native plants in Ohio. Just looking at the photo, I want to walk up the generous native stone steps and take a seat. Native plants provide screening in this corner of the yard. The slight change in elevation between the two seating areas creates a feeling of privacy. They have used two native trees, the ornamental serviceberry (*Amelanchier* species) and swamp white oak (*Quercus bicolor*). The perennials include asters (*Symphyotrichum* species) and sedum (*Sedum* species) (photo 29).

I worked on a new home in Iowa that clearly needed a landscape to create a welcoming appearance. It was a large brick house with a high, recessed entry porch. I designed a pergola to bring the entry down to human proportions and a limestone raised bed to add soft colors and shapes along the foundation. We used native limestone and concrete edging pavers and stepping-stones. I combined native and nonnative plants on this site with a high deer population. The plants include Gro-Low fragrant sumac (*Rhus aromatica* 'Gro-Low'), spiked gayfeather (*Liatris spicata*), Walker's Low catmint (*Nepeta racemosa* 'Walker's Low'), garden peony (*Paeonia* species), Husker Red penstemon (*Penstemon digitalis* 'Husker Red'), little bluestem (*Schizachyrium scoparium*), and Culver's root (*Veronicastrum virginicum*) (photo 30).

From these examples it is clear that as homeowners we can plant gardens using native plants in our neighborhoods. Add these gardens together, and we are building habitat. We can use nonnative plants for their links to past gardens, beauty, and deer resistance but must remember that we also need to provide appropriate habitat for wildlife. Use the design basics explained in this chapter, and make a plan that will bring you successful results.

Chapter 5 presents ideas on combining plants, how to use native plants with ones you know well. Designers from around the Midwest show us examples of more entries and borders. Look at these gardens with the knowledge about design you have learned in this chapter.

5

Combining Plants

Since the start of the twenty-first century, finding native plants for gardens has gone from difficult to easy. Now garden centers carry a wide variety of native grasses and wildflowers for the gardener. Landscape designers and contractors have a greater choice by ordering directly from the growers. I can select from hundreds of grasses and wildflowers from nurseries in the Midwest growing midwestern natives.

Sources of Plants and Seeds

Growers produce these plants in various sizes: plugs, flats, and pots. Plugs are grown thirty-two or thirty-eight in a flat (approximately ten × twenty inches). The best ones have deep cells and grow plants with vigorous roots and matching top growth. Flats are also available with ten to twelve plants. Individual pots are available up to gallon size. The availability of native trees and shrubs has improved as well.

Where does the seed come from? Hopefully the seed is collected from plants growing in the Midwest and even in areas close to where I am planning a garden. Then I know I am re-creating the habitat that has been lost, and the plants will thrive. When designers reconstruct prairies, woodlands, and savannas or restore remnants, the sources of seed and plants are critical and carry more parameters. They specify that the plants harvested for the seed must come from an ecotype that originates no more than fifty to one hundred miles from their planting area. An ecotype is the geological and environmental origin of the plant (where it evolved in nature). According to Greg Houseal, the project manager for Natural Selections Seed at the Tallgrass Prairie Center at the University of Northern Iowa, "Pooling seed collected from different populations in a defined area or region is a reasonable strategy for increasing genetic diversity." Carl Kurtz writes in *A Practical Guide to Prairie Reconstruction*, "that species diversity is more important than local-ecotype seed."

When we buy native plants from local nurseries, their sources are usually midwestern suppliers. When we order from midwestern catalogs, we buy plants grown in the Midwest. However, when ordering from catalogs from other states, it is much less likely that we get a Midwest-grown plant or seed. I have listed midwestern sources, both retail and wholesale, in the back of this book. We use seed when planting a large area or doing native reconstructions. For residential landscapes, I will use plant sizes ranging from plugs to one-gallon pots. I have had great success planting high-quality plugs of native plants and try to avoid the more expensive gallon pots, as there is not a benefit in terms of ultimate plant performance.

Native Cultivars

Another subject may cause some discussion as well. That is the use of native cultivars, or "nativars," a term coined by horticulturist and author Allan Armitage. Cultivars are selected and cultivated by humans. Nativars are cultivars of native plants. They, like all cultivars, must be propagated vegetatively through cuttings, grafting, or tissue culture. Propagation by seed usually produces something different from the parent plant. Cultivars have been selected for desirable characteristics such as color, height, bloom time and duration, and habit. The ecological value of cultivars bred from natives is not known because very little research has been done in this area. These plants may not support biodiversity. Some readily available nativars are Northwind switch grass (*Panicum virgatum* 'Northwind'), the shrub Summer Wine ninebark (*Physocarpus opulifolia* 'Seward'), and the small tree Autumn Brilliance serviceberry (*Amelanchier × grandiflora* 'Autumn Brilliance').

When reading plant labels or listings in a plant catalog, you will know that a plant with a botanical name in single quotation marks or preceded by the abbreviation "cv." is a cultivar or nativar. Botanical names, unlike common names (which often are not plant specific), tell us the genealogy of plants so we know just what we are buying. An example of a common name used for different plants is coneflower. Many species in the genus *Rudbeckia* are known in the vernacular as coneflowers. These include *Rudbeckia fulgida* and *R. subtomentosa*, both called coneflowers and black-eyed Susans. *Ratibida hirta* is also called a coneflower. The purple coneflower is *Echinacea purpurea*. *Ratibida pinnata* is a plant with a number of common names, including gray-headed coneflower, yellow coneflower, and prairie coneflower. I use all of these plants in my designs. My contractor needs to know which plants to order.

In *Armitage's Native Plants for North American Gardens* Armitage writes that "garden-improved cultivars, both selections and hybrids, will only help mainstream gardeners further embrace the world of native plants." This is a view held by many horticulturists and designers. They believe that the availability of nativars will inform more gardeners about native plants. Homeowners will see them in garden centers, be drawn to their beauty, and begin learning about the origin and ecological benefits of these plants.

Mike Yanny of Johnson's Nursery in Menomonee Falls, Wisconsin, offers both natives and nativars in his catalog. He believes that nativars can be the hook that gets gardeners interested in native plants.

When choosing plants to breed and sell, he considers desirable traits and selects for them. When asked if nativars serve the diverse needs of insects, he answers that it depends on the genotype, the complete heritable genetic identity. He writes, "Nativars are an important aspect of this education of the public. They are the WOW! plants of our native flora."

Neil Diboll of Prairie Nursery in Westfield, Wisconsin, decided not to offer nativars through his catalog "since our primary goal is ecological restoration using open-pollinated native plants." He adds, "The theory is that by using 'wild' plants we can preserve the genetic diversity of their gene pools." You will see his projects in chapter 6.

Doug Tallamy asks, when we select for height or another characteristic, what happens to insect diversity if the height of a plant determines how it is used as a food source? If birds or insects find a plant (as a food source or for habitat) by its height and we breed a shorter, more compact version for the garden, will the wildlife still find it? This is an ongoing discussion among horticulturists and breeders for gardeners and designers to recognize. It is agreed that more research is needed in this area.

Selecting Plants

Gardeners enjoy choosing plants to group for the greatest impact. We look forward to the beauty that will fill our landscape. Making your own combinations becomes the most enjoyable part of gardening, especially when you have a plan and know the plant will be going into the right place. Knowing which plants grew well together in a natural setting helps us choose plants for our gardens. These plant communities are tried-and-true. Is the area hot and dry or shady and moist, in sun or shade or partial shade? Does the soil drain well, or does it stay wet after a rain? Is the soil sandy or clayey? Is it a new bed or one that has been amended with organic matter over many years? The answers to these questions help us choose plants that will thrive.

I have tried many plants in my gardens and my clients' gardens, but still only a small sample of the possibilities. One of my favorite native plants is Culver's root (*Veronicastrum virginicum*) for its slender form and delicate white flower. It never interferes and sometimes can even get lost in the jumble of plants. Pale purple coneflower (*Echinacea pallida*) draws my interest with its tall stems and delicate pale purple petals. A grass, side oats grama (*Bouteloua curtipendula*), has copper-red seed heads that hang from curved stems. I have found switch grass (*Panicum virgatum*) aggressive, making its way through the beds. Little bluestem (*Schizachyrium scoparium*) flops in rich soils. I love false blue indigo (*Baptisia australis*) with its blue flowers in the spring and shrublike form. Seedpods hang from the stems in the fall and winter. I use prairie dropseed (*Sporobolus heterolepis*) everywhere, and it almost always grows larger than I expected.

In *Gardens in the Spirit of Place* Page Dickey discusses a geographical range of American gardens. These gardeners chose plants that will thrive within the ecological limits of each environment without needing excessive care, are not invasive, and seem appropriate to their settings in habit and character. She writes that gardens like these offer a "satisfying calmness achieved by plantings that blend with the natural landscape." Dickey recognizes a "new, nationwide reverence for the prairie's brilliantly colored, drought-tolerant, winter-hardy, butterfly-attracting summer flowers, as well as a growing appreciation of self-sustaining native plant communities."

Designed Gardens

The projects in this chapter represent design examples to encourage the reader to begin to use native plants. Nonnative plants and nativars appear in these gardens as well. Many designers today are combining these plants to achieve a desired aesthetic, to create deer-resistant gardens, to use plants suitable to the site, and to encourage gardeners to use native plants. A number of creative and knowledgeable designers and gardeners have shared their gardens with me. These examples provide numerous ideas.

31. Naturalistic plantings of large swaths of perennials and grasses require a detailed planting plan. Photo by Roy Diblik.

Roy Diblik co-owns Northwind Perennial Farm in Burlington, Wisconsin. His garden designs emphasize plant relationships. His work includes the Louis Sullivan Arch Garden for the Modern Wing at the Art Institute of Chicago and the lake plantings for the Oceanarium at Chicago's Shedd Aquarium. In his book *The Know Maintenance Perennial Garden*, Diblik writes that many ecologically planned native plantings lack an artistic vision. He uses combinations of native plants and dependable perennials for all of his work to create well-designed landscapes.

Diblik excels at creating large plantings of nonnatives in a naturalistic style; the ones shown here are from Wisconsin gardens. The

32. A variety of vertical and horizontal shapes creates a dynamic and beautiful landscape. Photo by Roy Diblik.

plants drift and repeat in a manner seen in nature (photo 31). In this large public garden he has used six kinds of plants, but in a smaller garden you can achieve the same effect using fewer varieties. He has included Hummelo lamb's ears (*Stachys officinalis* 'Hummelo'), Karl Foerster feather reed grass (*Calamagrostis × acutiflora* 'Karl Foerster'), Dropmore catmint (*Nepeta × faassenii* 'Dropmore'), Russian sage (*Perovskia atriplicifolia*), calaminth (*Calamintha nepeta* ssp. *nepeta*), and Happy Returns daylily (*Hemerocallis* 'Happy Returns'). Another of Diblik's projects shows a more complex combination of native and non-native plants (photo 32). Here large drifts of grasses combine with smaller groups of perennials. The striking composition includes Gold

33. Lines of trees and groups of perennials lead visitors to a building. Photo by Roy Diblik.

Dew tufted hair grass (*Deschampsia* 'Goldtau'), blazing star (*Liatris spicata*), Tara prairie dropseed (*Sporobolus heterolepis* 'Tara'), and Purple Candles astilbe (*Astilbe chinensis* 'Purpurkurze'). The mood of this landscape contrasts with that of the previous one to show the wide range of effects possible using this rich palette of plants. They punctuate the design, commanding the visitor to look.

In a project for another public building Diblik again uses bands of color, this time with less variation, with Blue Fortune anise hyssop (*Agastache* 'Blue Fortune'), Virgin coneflower (*Echinacea purpurea* 'Virgin'), and Bowman's root (*Porteranthus trifoliatus*) (photo 33). The last, less common plant is native to parts of the Midwest. The garden, along

34. Groups of perennials and grasses show their colors in the fall. Photo by Roy Diblik.

a walkway, illustrates how a planting can lead a viewer or visitor up to an entrance of a building. It creates a pleasant journey, encouraging close observation of the environment. One of the major considerations of a landscape designer is how people navigate a garden. Plants make that process clearer and add a sensory element as we see, touch, and smell them.

Designers consider the color, shape, and form of plants in four seasons, particularly in the Midwest where we experience them all. Diblik shows us the beauty of perennials in the fall: Karl Foerster feather reed grass (*Calamagrostis × acutiflora* 'Karl Foerster'), Blue Paradise phlox (*Phlox paniculata* 'Blue Paradise'), Golden Showers coreopsis (*Coreop-*

35. A lively group of perennials and grasses includes purple coneflower (*Echinacea purpurea*), autumn moor grass (*Sesleria autumnalis*), and Northwind switch grass (*Panicum virgatum* 'Northwind'). Photo by Roy Diblik.

sis verticillata 'Golden Showers'), wild quinine (*Parthenium integrifolium*), Pixie Meadowbrite coneflower (*Echinacea* 'Pixie Meadowbrite'), autumn moor grass (*Sesleria autumnalis*), and prairie dropseed (*Sporobolus heterolepis*) (photo 34). I leave my garden plants standing throughout the fall. Perennials, not only trees and shrubs, create color in the autumn garden. They also continue to provide habitat.

Another of Diblik's designs uses grasses and perennials planted at the base of a tree. This garden runs along the side of a building and turns what would be a dull area into one that draws the interest of the passerby. Commonly, one would see a monoculture row of a single variety of shrub surrounded by mulch with a strip of lawn. Diblik's plant palette allows his imagination to amaze us. Autumn moor grass (*Sesleria autumnalis*) wanders through a planting of Hummelo lamb's

36. The orange of Moerheim Beauty sneezeweed (*Helenium* 'Moerheim Beauty') and white of White Swan coneflower (*Echinacea purpurea* 'White Swan') bring this planting to life. Photo by Adam Woodruff.

ears (*Stachys officinalis* 'Hummelo'), willow leaf blue star (*Amsonia tabernaemontana*), purple coneflower (*Echinacea purpurea*), Northwind switch grass (*Panicum virgatum* 'Northwind'), and flat-topped aster (*Doellingeria umbellata*) (photo 35).

Adam Woodruff, who owns Adam Woodruff + Associates in St. Louis, Missouri, works in the same context as Roy Diblik. Woodruff combines herbaceous and woody plants, both native and nonnative, to form a tapestry of yearlong interest. His Jones Road project in Missouri provided the homeowners with a beautiful composition that blends with the surrounding natural area.

Photographs of this project show creative combinations of native plants, nativars, and nonnative plants. Woodruff chose a group of plants for what I would call an exciting design (photo 36). The variety

37. Small repeating groups of perennials mingle and are tied together throughout by autumn moor grass (*Sesleria autumnalis*). Photo by Adam Woodruff.

of flower shapes—spiky, cone-shaped, and flat—makes the scene alive, and it is easy to imagine the sound of bees. The orange *Helenium* punctuates the picture, adding surprise to the blues, whites, and greens. The plants include Moerheim Beauty sneezeweed (*Helenium* 'Moerheim Beauty'), Rosea Culver's root (*Veronicastrum virginicum* 'Rosea'), White Swan coneflower (*Echinacea purpurea* 'White Swan'), prairie dock (*Silphium terebinthinaceum*), and Russian sage (*Perovskia atriplicifolia*).

Another grouping, in a more subdued mood, would fit into many gardens and shows well-known plants forming a pleasing composition (photo 37). Here round and cone-shaped flowers dominate, and spiky grasses support the composition. The large leaves of the alumroot have a calming effect. Woodruff repeats groups of Kim's Knee High

38. Both large and narrow leaves of perennials and grasses create a highly textural landscape in summer. Photo by Adam Woodruff.

39. The scene repeats in fall when the grasses take over the show and echo the stance of the sculpture. Photo by Adam Woodruff.

coneflower (*Echinacea purpurea* 'Kim's Knee High'), ornamental allium (*Allium* species), alumroot (*Heuchera villosa*), calaminth (*Calamintha nepeta* ssp. *nepeta*), and autumn moor grass (*Sesleria autumnalis*). The now common coneflower never fails to delight the viewer.

A large grouping around the pool consists of swaths of plants that intermingle at the edges (photo 38). The leaves of grasses and perennials create a composition of texture with flowers as accent: prairie dock (*Silphium terebinthinaceum*), White Swan coneflower (*Echinacea purpurea* 'White Swan'), Russian sage (*Perovskia atriplicifolia*), and prairie dropseed (*Sporobolus heterolepis*). Woodruff has softened the combination close to the pool, making the landscape comfortable for the swimmers. Landscape designers use plants with soft textures, modest heights, and pleasant scents around patios and pools. Looking at a photo of the same area in the fall allows us to compare the scenes (photo 39). One is a canvas of greens; the other, of browns and tans. In the fall the grasses dominate the view. Leaving spent plants standing in the garden in the fall and winter provides cover and food for wildlife and a beautiful scene, with or without snow.

In my designs, both for clients and for my own garden, I use combinations of native and nonnative plants, trees, shrubs, perennials, and grasses. These combinations create beauty, habitat, and, when necessary, deer-resistant gardens. Over time I have learned how to combine the plants and find ones suitable for each situation. I must admit that I will buy a plant simply for the beauty of its blooms and then have difficulty placing it in my garden. It is far better to find a place in the garden where new plants could be added and then design a combination for the space. Each project improves the next one. I will return to a site and make adjustments, just as gardeners do in their gardens. Although I do not adhere to the rule that taller plants must always be placed at the back of a bed, there are times when perennials have not grown as I had expected and I need to shift their positions in a garden.

Using a mixture of small trees, shrubs, grasses, and perennials allows me to move away from the convention of foundation plantings. When the garden begins at the house and moves toward the sidewalk

40. In summer an entry planting in a deer-resistant garden fills the bed with perennials, grasses, shrubs, and an ornamental tree.

41. In fall a different palette of plants puts on a show and includes a sedge and two varieties of catmint.

and street, it connects the house to the land. The buildings appear to grow out of the ground. Less lawn to maintain and mow adds a benefit.

One project in Cedar Rapids contains native and nonnative plants with deer resistance as the top priority. New subdivisions in former natural areas have a high deer population, which does damage that often cannot be repaired. On this site a deer family makes its home in the backyard. In a photo taken in summer these plants are blooming: Moonshine yarrow (*Achillea millifolium* 'Moonshine'), common spiderwort (*Tradescantia ohiensis*), and foxglove beardtongue (*Penstemon digitalis*) (photo 40). The same scene in a photo taken in early fall (photo 41) shows the additional plants blue sedge (*Carex flacca*), northern sea oats (*Chasmanthium latifolium*), Walker's Low catmint (*Nepeta racemosa* 'Walker's Low'), Kit Kat catmint (*N. × faassenii* 'Kit Kat'), Goldsturm black-eyed Susan (*Rudbeckia fulgida* 'Goldsturm'), and Indian grass (*Sorghastrum nutans*). These two areas flank the front entry to the home, creating an unusual landscape for that neighborhood. The plantings soften the long concrete steps and large porch. Visitors enjoy a sensory experience. One thing I have learned working as a landscape designer is that I can never take too many photos of projects. When I find the same scene in more than one photo, I am delighted and remind myself to be sure to photograph in all seasons. Doing so is certainly worth the time and fuel. The photo is only one moment in the long life of a garden. The value of the garden is the hours it is inhabited.

On the sloped yard of this home, big bluestem (*Andropogon gerardii*) and Shenandoah switch grass (*Panicum virgatum* 'Shenandoah') lean in the direction the house faces (photo 42), accentuating the prairie-style architecture of the house. Many newer homes in the Midwest use this style, and I have enjoyed designing gardens for some of them. Native gardens easily replace traditional foundation plantings in these landscapes. This garden eliminated mowing the hill with the added benefit that rainwater enters the ground and does not run off into the street and storm sewer. The homeowners wanted less lawn to maintain in addition to a deer-resistant landscape. The mixture of native and nonnative grasses, flowers, shrubs, and trees gave them four seasons of interest.

42. Graceful grasses move in the breeze, softening the hard lines of the house and connecting it to the landscape.

43. This garden screens a view of the patio area from the road with a combination of mainly native plants, including the white-spired Album Culver's root (*Veronicastrum virginicum* 'Album').

44. This view from the patio includes bright Peter Pan goldenrod (*Solidago* 'Peter Pan') and Golden Glory cornelian cherry dogwood (*Cornus mas* 'Golden Glory').

In my landscape at home we removed an old privet hedge along the driveway and replaced it with a low-maintenance mixed bed of perennials, small trees, shrubs, and grasses. The hedge had required yearly pruning. The garden partially screens our patio from the road. See-through screens add a lovely dimension to a landscape. We gain some privacy but do not lose the views beyond the garden. This screen utilizes a group of native plants that I moved from another part of the yard. Here they shine. One view is from the driveway (photo 43), and the other is from patio side (photo 44). The plants include Peter Pan goldenrod (*Solidago* 'Peter Pan'), Album Culver's root (*Veronicastrum virginicum* 'Album'), little bluestem (*Schizachyrium scoparium*), Gro-Low fragrant sumac (*Rhus aromatica* 'Gro-Low'), Autumn Joy sedum (*Sedum* 'Autumn Joy'), Platinum Blue globe thistle (*Echinops ritro* 'Platinum Blue'), Golden Spirit smokebush (*Cotinus coggygria* 'Golden Spirit'), and Golden Glory cornelian cherry dogwood (*Cornus mas* 'Golden Glory'). The dogwood serves as a marker when pulling into and out

45. Although less dense, the garden in the fall continues to screen the road with leaves of orange, red, brown, and yellow.

of the driveway and prevents us from driving over the garden. The color combinations in the late summer and fall when the dogwood and sumac leaves turn shades of orange and red and the perennials glow with warm browns and yellows add to our enjoyment of the garden (photo 45).

The projects in this chapter demonstrate the possibilities of including native plants in your gardens whether large or small. These designers used the same design considerations all gardeners rely on. They thought about color, form, and texture. They noted movement, both of those walking by or through the garden and of the plants in the wind. They created repeating groups of plants that reflect how plant communities thrive in undisturbed areas. Most important, they created gardens to be enjoyed by clients or themselves and habitat for wildlife.

Chapter 6 presents projects of native landscapes and shows how they can work, even in a residential environment.

6

Residential Prairies and Woodlands

Unlike large prairie reconstructions and remnant restorations, prairies planted around homes in residential landscapes are part of a designed landscape plan. Although part of a residential landscape, they are smaller prairie reconstructions, a chance to return a piece of the tallgrass prairie to the landscape. Daryl Smith of the University of Northern Iowa writes about this process in a chapter of *The Tallgrass Prairie Center Guide to Prairie Restoration in the Upper Midwest*. As we view photographs or, even better, the sites in person, we are introduced to the idea of using natives in this way. The familiarity of a residential setting (we can see parts of homes or other structures) creates a comfort zone for the viewer. The use of prairie becomes plausible and possible.

Planning

Why are designers and homeowners planting prairie in their landscape? The answer is many of the reasons discussed earlier in this book. These plantings evoke the past landscape and contribute to the sustainability of the plan. They help keep rainwater on-site and reduce erosion by using plants whose roots grow deep into the soil. They eliminate or lessen the use of herbicides, pesticides, and fertilizers and the frequency of mowing. They create habitat for a diverse population of insects, butterflies, birds, and mammals.

In addition, these prairies are stunning. The plants follow the contour of the land and sway with the wind, bringing movement to the landscape. The shape of their leaves and colors of their flowers collect water and attract insects, respectively, while we enjoy the view. They change through the seasons as different wildflowers emerge, grow tall, and bloom and a variety of grasses sprout, reach great heights, and produce distinct seed heads.

Residential prairies require planning, correct planting methods, and wise management. They have acquired a poor image from the many front yards planted to prairie without the necessary design, horticultural, and maintenance knowledge. These yards become a statement rather than a beautiful living space. Homeowners have been encouraged to use native plants for the ecological reasons I have discussed. These attempts may show the gardeners believe that planting a prairie is the only way to garden sustainably. Planting a prairie is not as simple as planting a lawn. I think we can have both a beautiful and a sustainable native landscape.

Before you plant a residential prairie, the existing vegetation, whether weeds or sod, must be removed. In large areas, spraying with a nonselective, nonresidual herbicide such as glyphosate is most practical. In small areas, you can remove the existing sod or smother it with newspapers or plastic. Whatever method is used, if time permits, leave the area alone for a couple of weeks and then remove any weeds that regrow before planting. The remaining dead roots will add organic matter to the soil. There is no need to till; just mow the remaining dead sod very close to the soil surface and rake off the debris to create a seedbed for the prairie mix. Broadcast the seed, and then press it into the ground with a roller. Prairie seed needs close contact with the ground and should not be covered with soil. Chapter 7 discusses this process in more detail.

Before choosing the seed mix, consider the needs of the site and the design. Will the area receive sun or shade? What is the soil type? Do you require visibility or screening? Are you interested in an expanse of many different types of flowers and grasses or a broad swath of three to five species? Are there city, county, or subdivision codes regulating weeds and plant height? Municipalities and neighbors may object to tall prairie plants. People are used to seeing yards with lawns and are comfortable with their appearance. A weed-free green, bluegrass lawn to them means being a good neighbor. To the uninformed, prairie plants are weeds, particularly when they are tall and fall over onto sidewalks and driveways. In addition cities write codes that state how high plants may be along intersections so they do not hinder visibility and create unsafe driving conditions. Investigate the rules and educate your neighbors. Design a residential prairie that will work for the site. A mowed strip around the perimeter of a prairie gives the landscape a neat and well-planned appearance.

Designed Landscapes

Clients of mine in Iowa built a house on a corner lot in a subdivision. The lot had a small level area in the front yard and a swale along the street and then became steep and wooded behind the house. They built right up to the woods and wanted no landscaping in back. From the start the idea was to surround a small lawn with a shortgrass prairie. The subdivision had no sidewalks, so the lawns ran to the street through the swale in the right-of-way. I designed the prairie to encircle and hug the lawn and small landscaped beds. We killed the existing old pasture, broadcast the prairie seed, and laid erosion mat on the swale.

I began the design work in 2010, and the crew planted the prairie in 2011. Each year we examined the seedlings, seeking to identify prairie plants, and each year we found more. We had two years of drought, but by 2014 the prairie had filled in beautifully. The homeowners did all of the maintenance, weeding, and mowing and added seed as needed.

46. Seen from the street, this young prairie covers the sloped yard with yellow gray-headed coneflower (*Ratibida pinnata*) and a few foxglove beardtongue (*Penstemon digitalis*).

Behind the house in an area disturbed by construction, we planted a low-growing fescue that needs little if any mowing. We ordered the seed from Ion Exchange in Harpers Ferry, Iowa. For the prairie we used their Dry Site/Short Prairie Seed Mix, and for the slope behind the house we used their No-Mow/Low-Grow Lawn Seed (photos 46–48).

Another client of mine in Iowa had developed a deep interest in native plants. She wanted a prairie planted on a slope in her backyard. We met, and I suggested a native garden of shrubs, ornamental trees, wildflowers, and grasses. We used plugs for the prairie native flowers and grasses. In just the second year after planting, the garden is a diverse mixture of plants with varying heights, forms, colors, and habits. In subsequent years it will improve and become denser. We

47. The house and deck, snug against the woods, face the bright, sunny prairie. The landscape transitions from a small ornamental planting to lawn to prairie.

48. The homeowner saved this native pin oak (*Quercus palustris*) when the house was built. We see how the prairie circles the lawn and how this landscape enhances the neighborhood.

49. I used prairie plant plugs, arranging them in groups that repeat throughout the garden. The shrub, bush honeysuckle (*Diervilla lonicera*), and the outcropping limestone add structure to the landscape.

added native outcropping limestone to help hold the slope. In summer the garden fills with prairie plants that grow together into a delightful bouquet (photo 49). The plants include lance-leaf tickseed (*Coreopsis lanceolata*), foxglove beardtongue (*Penstemon digitalis*), Culver's root (*Veronicastrum virginicum*), prairie dropseed (*Sporobolus heterolepis*), and bush honeysuckle (*Diervilla lonicera*). Here the use of the botanical name is particularly important because this last plant is not related to the honeysuckle that invades woodlands. Using native shrubs in the garden adds structure and interest. At the beginning of fall we can catch the beauty of the grasses, northern sea oats (*Chasmanthium latifolium*) and side oats grama (*Bouteloua curtipendula*), as they turn shades from rust to brown (photos 50–51).

I designed a prairie planting for a cemetery in Iowa, a different kind of residence. The congregation had enlarged the cemetery. In addition

50. The sculptural quality of northern sea oats (*Chasmanthium latifolium*) stands up to the solid presence of the limestone.

51. The wide variety of leaf and flower shapes and growth habits of prairie plants create habitat and food sources for a diverse group of insects and butterflies.

52. This large area of young prairie covers ground that will be used for cemetery burial space many years from now. A circle driveway curves through the prairie.

53. Limestone cubes provide seating on the patio under vintage oak trees. Evening primrose (*Oenothera biennis*) joins black-eyed Susan (*Rudbeckia hirta*) in the prairie.

54. This project on Neil Diboll's acreage shows a prairie thriving on what was once a field of invasive and undesirable trees and shrubs. Photo by Neil Diboll, Prairie Nursery of Westfield, Wisconsin.

to a new patio and seating area, I added the prairie where burials will happen many years in the future. The new area had been cleared of trees, backfilled with poor soil, and planted to grass. The poor soil provided a suitable site to introduce prairie plants. We used a Dry Site/ Short Prairie Seed Mix from Ion Exchange. In just its first year after planting, the prairie makes a statement and enhances the peaceful and meditative site. Young prairies usually are predominantly yellow with black-eyed Susan (*Rudbeckia hirta*) (photos 52–53). In future years many additional plants will germinate and fill the area. The contractor weeded the new planting and burned it the first spring.

Neil Diboll, who owns Prairie Nursery in Westfield, Wisconsin, is an internationally recognized expert in the field of ecological and natural landscape design and installation. Diboll has generously sent me photos of their residential prairie projects. Their catalog states that "each

55. A prairie covers a septic field, providing a low-maintenance and beautiful option for a difficult area. Photo by Neil Diboll, Prairie Nursery of Westfield, Wisconsin.

yard is an important link, connected to a growing network of native plant gardens that support life across urban and rural landscapes."

Diboll planted a front yard prairie on his acreage (photo 54). Box elder (*Acer negundo*), glossy buckthorn (*Rhamnus frangula*), and Tatarian honeysuckle (*Lonicera tatarica*) had filled this area. The first two plants, a tree and a shrub, are aggressive native plants, and the third is an invasive nonnative that has naturalized in woodlands. He cut everything down; sprayed with glyphosate, a herbicide, three times a year for two years; and hand-broadcast the seed in the fall onto the bare soil. The seed worked its way into the soil by means of the natural frost action of the ground over the winter and early spring. The plants include butterfly weed (*Asclepias tuberosa*), black-eyed Susan (*Rudbeckia hirta*), wild quinine (*Parthenium integrifolium*), foxglove beardtongue (*Penstemon digitalis*), and pale purple coneflower (*Echinacea pallida*).

56. The front entry of a house is enhanced by a prairie full of flowers, creating a lovely view of the landscape from the porch. Photo by Neil Diboll, Prairie Nursery of Westfield, Wisconsin.

At a rural home in Wisconsin, the homeowners installed a new septic field. They seeded Prairie Nursery's Septic Field Prairie Mix right onto the sand and gravel that were used to backfill the septic field. Because the species in this mix are adapted to growing in low-nutrient sandy soils, they thrived. The sand and gravel came from an underground glacial deposit and were essentially weed-free. Many midwesterners live in subdivisions and on acreages and farms with septic fields. The only choice to cover these areas has been lawn grass, which often grows with thin or bare patches in these situations. Using a septic prairie mixture could be a better choice. The dominant flowers in this project are lupine (*Lupinus perennis*) and lanceleaf tickseed (*Coreopsis lanceolata*) (photo 55).

This next Diboll project is a prairie garden, also in Wisconsin. The owner burns it every year (photo 56). The flowers in this planting were

57. Here another prairie fits successfully into a residential neighborhood and supplies habitat for more than one yard. Photo by Neil Diboll, Prairie Nursery of Westfield, Wisconsin.

installed by the owner using transplants. The plants include purple coneflower (*Echinacea purpurea*), brown-eyed Susan (*Rudbeckia triloba*), black-eyed Susan (*R. hirta*), prairie dropseed (*Sporobolus heterolepis*), and little bluestem (*Schizachyrium scoparium*). This landscape illustrates a native planting working very well as a front garden.

In a suburban Wisconsin neighborhood, Diboll designed the seed mix used to establish this prairie in the owner's side yard, which adjoins the driveway of a neighbor who was very happy to have the prairie abutting his property. The prairie owner kept an area of bluegrass lawn directly in front of the house. His goal was to provide food and cover for birds. The project in its third year includes gray-headed coneflower (*Ratibida pinnata*), black-eyed Susan (*Rudbeckia hirta*), bergamot (*Monarda fistulosa*), and purple prairie clover (*Dalea purpurea*) (photo 57).

The design/build firm Salsbury-Schweyer, Inc., of Akron, Ohio, creates sustainable landscapes, including prairie reconstructions. One home on a large property looks out on an expansive prairie, providing wonderful views in all seasons. Here we see the prairie in summer and fall. The grassy area that curves through the prairie is Prairie Nursery's No Mow Lawn Seed Mix, a low-growing fescue. The flowering plants include butterfly weed (*Asclepias tuberosa*) and pale purple coneflower (*Echinacea pallida*). The prairie mix contains about thirty grasses and flowers (photos 58–59).

Since 1992, Mark Müller and Valerie Cool have developed their acreage in eastern Iowa into a wonderland of prairie, pond, and gardens. Their prairie surrounds the pond and includes mowed paths for easy circulation. Surrounded by agricultural fields, their prairie creates a home for a diverse group of insects and birds and people, as the homeowners always welcome visitors. Müller and Cool have more than four hundred native species on four acres. The seed for the oldest plantings came from Ion Exchange in 1993. Müller also used seed he collected locally from cemeteries and roadsides and from Carl Kurtz, a photographer who has worked to reconstruct prairies in Iowa. Müller has drawn beautiful botanical illustrations of native plants for posters produced by Iowa's Living Roadway Trust Fund.

Müller and Cool enjoy sunsets from a restored outbuilding on the property at one end of the pond. The plants include arrowhead (*Sagittaria latifolia*), rose mallow (*Hibiscus laevis*), cardinal flower (*Lobelia cardinalis*), indigo bush (*Amorpha fruticosa*), and wool grass (*Scirpus cyperinus*) (photo 60). Another photo of the pond and prairie (photo 61) includes additional wetland plants: swamp milkweed (*Asclepias incarnata*), ironweed (*Vernonia fasciculata*), water hemlock (*Cicuta maculata*), sweetflag (*Acorus calamus*), cordgrass (*Spartina pectinata*), blueflag iris (*Iris virginica* var. *shrevei*), and sedges (*Carex* species). Wetland species provide a diverse palette of prairie plants that have adapted to periods of submersion. Use them in the center of rain gardens and in low, wet areas of a yard. Some, such as cordgrass, sedges, and ironweed, in addition to growing in wet soil, will grow in moist soil, so they can be

58. A summer view of a large prairie invites the visitor to walk around the bend to the home. Photo by Salsbury-Schweyer, Inc.

59. Prairie landscapes provide impressive views in the fall and summer, as well as much less maintenance than lawn. Photo by Salsbury-Schweyer, Inc.

60. A refurbished farm building, a pond, farm fields, native prairie, established trees, and farmyard together create an idyllic midwestern scene. Photo by Mark Müller.

61. A pond with native wetland plant species, surrounded by prairie and agricultural lands, draws waterfowl, birds, insects, butterflies, and people to enjoy the habitat.

62. A prairie, established over twenty years ago, reclaims land that held row crops and now offers a place to stroll.

used in native gardens in the landscape. The view of the prairie with the cornfields beyond includes buttonbush (*Cephalanthus occidentalis*), partridge pea (*Chamaecrista fasciculata*), big bluestem (*Andropogon gerardii*), and Indian grass (*Sorghastrum nutans*) (photo 62).

My husband and I began to plant areas of prairie more than twenty years ago as well. We now have about one-third acre plus our ditch in prairie. Surrounded by corn and soybean fields, our prairies reflect the contours of the land and the expanse of sky. As we walk through them on mown paths, the loud sounds of insects drown out any noise of vehicles on the gravel road. As we learned more, we began to order our seed from the Ion Exchange in Harpers Ferry, choosing tallgrass prairie mixes. The mixes contained both flowers and grasses, but we found that the flowers dominated the plantings, so we began to order additional native grass seed.

63. Looking north across the prairie toward the house, we see gray-headed coneflower (*Ratibida pinnata*) and wild bergamot (*Monarda fistulosa*). The movement of the clouds accentuates the contours of the land, how it dips and then rises again.

64. Paths through the prairie draw in the curious visitor. In the distance, through the trees, the white hay barn connects visually with the white fence. Cup plant (*Silphium perfoliatum*) joins the mix.

65. Our prairie in late summer showcases yellow goldenrod (*Solidago* species), spent coneflower seed heads, and Canada wild rye (*Elymus canadensis*). The upright, spiky plants intersect the gentle contours of our pasture and the neighbor's soybean field.

66. In winter the dormant prairie maintains its upward stance against the snow-covered pasture and cropland.

67. On early-morning walks through the prairie, I find numerous spider webs. Here, a spider wove its web between big bluestem (*Andropogon gerardii*) and sweet black-eyed Susan (*Rudbeckia subtomentosa*).

We initially removed the sod to prepare areas for seeding. For later projects we sprayed with glyphosate. This was less laborious, and we are not left with large quantities of sod to discard or compost. All of the topsoil remained on-site. We waited a couple of weeks and then resprayed or pulled new weeds. We then mowed the dead grass, raked it off, and broadcast the seed by hand. Mixing the seed with damp sand helps it fall to the ground and not blow away. We divided the sand/seed mixture into four parts, broadcasting the mixture four times, starting at a different place each time to be sure we covered the entire area.

When we bought the property, only a few trees and shrubs and a windbreak existed on the site. As a result we had no birds. As we made gardens and planted trees, birds began to visit us. It was after we had started our prairies that the birds and butterfly population greatly

68. The mayapple (*Podophyllum peltatum*) blossom hides beneath its large leaves in spring. This was the first wildflower I learned as a Girl Scout Brownie.

69. Common in woods, but nevertheless thrilling to find in spring, is the wild geranium (*Geranium maculatum*).

70. Another frequently found spring bloomer, wild blue phlox (*Phlox divaricata*), brightens the ground layer in woodlands.

increased. The prairies have decreased the amount of sloping lawn to mow. The landscape now provides beautiful and varied views of our prairies (photos 63–67). From summer through winter, they portray how the native plants create habitat for humans as well as butterflies, spiders, and other wildlife. We enjoy our prairies in all seasons.

The prairies reflect the horizon lines, cloud formations, and field and fence contours and frame views of buildings. They visually connect our built structures to the land. The verticality of the plants, how they reach to the sky, is a powerful image. As we added more plots of prairie, we left paths of grass to mow so we could easily visit and observe the plants and insects.

Although Iowa is known for its tallgrass prairies, woodlands also add to the landscape. Woodland remnants are found on ridges and

71. Joe Pye weed (*Eupatorium purpureum*) dots the Mutels' woods in early fall. Here a butterfly feeds.

ravines that could not be farmed. Homeowners fortunate to live in woods often can encourage the growth of native ground covers and manage the tree growth by burning rather than planting. Connie and Robert Mutel built their home in a woodland and manage the land with the goal of creating an environment where native woodland plants will thrive. I visited the woods in two seasons. In the spring I found three May bloomers, mayapple (*Podophyllum peltatum*), wild geranium (*Geranium maculatum*), and wild blue phlox (*Phlox divaricata*) (photos 68–70). In the fall I found Joe Pye weed (*Eupatorium purpureum*) (photos 71–72). A path leads from the house through the woodland. The Mutels burn a section of the woodland each year and manage the tree population by removing some trees and encouraging others to become mature.

Jack Pizzo of Pizzo and Associates in Illinois designs and installs natural and ecologically sound landscapes and also grows native

72. The Mutels sited their home where it becomes a part of the woodland. A narrow path leads into the woods.

plants at Pizzo Native Plant Nursery. They create, restore, and steward natural areas and manage native, sustainable landscapes. In one of Pizzo's projects, a large native planting meets the task of connecting the home to the site (photo 73). Plants include mountain mint (*Pycnanthemum* species), vervain (*Verbena* species), black-eyed Susan (*Rudbeckia hirta*), and switch grass (*Panicum* species). The large drifts of plants have a calming effect and create graceful movement in the landscape as well as leading our eyes toward the house. A patio with a stone wall provides a vantage point to observe lawn, prairie, and woods (photo 74). A native planting softens the edges of the stone: butterfly weed (*Asclepias tuberosa*), black-eyed Susan (*Rudbeckia hirta*), coreopsis (*Coreopsis* species), and beardtongue (*Penstemon* species).

In another Pizzo project, we see a house located on Lake Michigan with a boardwalk to the lake. The property is a birch–maple–bur oak savanna system with remnants. Weeds were removed and the savanna

73. Converting a front lawn into a prairie removes the maintenance of a lawn, saving time, money, and resources. This planting accentuates the architecture of the house far more successfully. Photo by Jack Pizzo.

74. The use of lawn here has the effect of making the prairie planting even more beautiful than perhaps a field of prairie would. Lawn does provide space for sports play and also for erecting tents for special occasions. Photo by Jack Pizzo.

75. Opening this woods and restoring the native ground layer created a wonderful view of the house. Photo by Jack Pizzo.

restored through burning. Trillium (*Trillium grandiflorum*) flowers bloom among little bluestem (*Schizachyrium scoparium*) and bloodroot (*Sanguinaria canadensis*) (photo 75). Since midwestern woodlands have not been degraded to the extent that prairies have, restoration of woodland species is often possible. These areas have been used for lumber or grazing of animals but have not been cultivated for crops or had heavy machinery compact the soils.

These native landscapes offer an alternative to conventional landscaping. They show beauty and a responsible approach to residential land use. The benefits to those living on these sites cannot be quantified but would be affirmed by the homeowners. I hope the sense of well-being derived from experiencing this environment will encourage more native landscaping.

7

Planting and Maintenance

I have included information about planning and planting gardens in the previous chapters. In this chapter, I explain in more detail the gardening part of using native plants in residential gardens. Some of my clients are experienced gardeners who have little need for the information sheets I provide about planting and maintenance. Others are new to gardening or know only enough to ask all the right questions. My readers probably fall into the same categories.

Much has been written about garden practices and prairie reconstruction. Here, I will share how I carry out these tasks at home and for my clients. Garden designers look at the entire landscape as a group of planned gardens that brings us outside to enjoy the beauty of the habitats we have created. Caring for the gardens is part of the plan. I will make the process as simple and commonsense as possible. Very often doing less and using fewer resources will give us more in return. Gardening is hard work. There are ways to minimize the burden, starting with making a plan that you can manage.

Probably, my favorite part of garden maintenance is the walk-through to assess what needs to be done. I take the opportunity to take close looks at the gardens to learn how each plant and area are doing. If I have been able to set aside a large chunk of time that day, I relish the thought of spending those hours in the garden without having to rush off to a meeting or other obligation.

Bed Preparation

Preparation for beds and borders and for native gardens starts with the same first step as for prairie reconstructions: removal of existing vegetation. For all gardens other than vegetable gardens, this is our only chance to prepare the soil by removing weeds and other undesirable plants. Take the time for thorough preparation. Effort now means less work as the garden matures.

Remove sod by digging and scraping it off (way too hard), using a rented sod cutter, covering the area with plastic or newspapers until the grass dies, or spraying with a glyphosate herbicide when planting a very large or weed-filled area. Renting a sod cutter means you will need a way to get it home and back and someone to run it. It is a heavy machine, so be prepared. When using materials like plastic sheets or newspapers to cover the lawn to kill it, you will have to wait longer for results—up to a month. You will probably have to do some hand-digging to remove persistent plants. If you prepare your garden in the fall, you will have a head start on the whole process the following spring. Remember, though, that the plastic-sheet method works best during the hot days of summer.

Using herbicides requires learning how to use the product. Landscape contractors need to have up-to-date certifications for its use. The herbicide will kill or damage any plants it contacts, so spray on a low-wind day. There will almost always be a breeze, so exercise caution and protect valuable plants by covering them or using barriers, such as large pieces of cardboard. Liz Maas, a restoration ecologist and biology instructor, suggests using a dye in the herbicide so that you can tell where you have sprayed. Follow all safety instructions on the container. When you buy the herbicide, also buy the appropriate sprayer, gloves, and eye protection. Keep your arms and legs covered.

I have colleagues who write and speak against this approach, but I feel that it uses the least resources. Ecologists and prairie managers I know and respect use this method. Glyphosate binds tightly to the soil, so little is transferred by rain or irrigation water to other locations or to the groundwater. Microbes in the soil break down the product. The time it takes for half of the product to break down ranges from 1 to 174 days. When I spray, I make sure to keep dogs and cats off the area until it is totally dry. I would keep children off until the foliage has died and the debris removed. I recommend this method for larger areas meant for native plants.

Soils have a large seed bank, seeds just waiting for the time to germinate. For this reason, when time permits, leave the new garden bare for two weeks and then remove additional weeds that have sprouted. Some people plan a year ahead, giving weed seeds time to germinate many times and removing them each time. The best time to seed a prairie is early summer, but the fall works as well. Dormant seeding, done after all chance of germination for that year is past, can be very successful. The seed has the time to make firm contact with the soil during the winter snows and freezing and thawing of the ground. Prairie seed can remain on the ground for a few years before germinating, and some young plants send down roots long before we see their leaves.

For perennial gardens, the next step is adding soil amendments such as compost and other organic matter. These materials add fertility and improve the texture of the soil. Texture refers to the size of the soil particles. We want our soils to hold moisture yet drain well. In sandy soils the particles are large, leaving spaces that allow water to drain away quickly. In clay soils the particles are small and bind together, retaining water and slowing drainage. Loam soil is a mixture of particle sizes, and it both lets water drain and remains moist for root intake of water. When we amend soils with organic matter, the soil becomes more like loam. In perennial gardens we want fertile, loamy soils. Most plants do well under these conditions.

When we established our borders at home, we began by removing the sod with a cutter. We used the sod in another part of the yard or composted it. We then rototilled the soil, adding in compost and peat. Over the years we have top-dressed the beds with compost and mulched them with shredded hardwood. As the beds filled with plants, they needed less mulch. Large plants shade the soil, preventing weed seed germination, and compete better with weeds. Over the years the beds became very rich, teeming with soil microbes and worms. After the initial addition of organic matter, I top-dress with compost, but I never use additional fertilizers. My gardens do not need them.

I have read about the depletion of peat sources and the recommendation not to use it. Peat producers do not agree. During the Garden Writers Association symposium in Quebec City in 2013, I visited a peat farm in Quebec, where some bogs are converted to wetlands after harvest and provide habitat for birds and plants. In addition, the peat farms are reestablishing peatlands by reintroducing peatland plant species to areas previously harvested. However, the restoration rate of bogs is very slow. The producers explain that they harvest only a small percentage of the available peat. Peatlands are ecosystems where the production of biomass exceeds its decomposition and therefore continues to increase, although slowly. The result is the accumulation of organic matter coming from plant debris over thousands of years. Gardeners have used peat for decades as a soil amendment. I now use less peat and more compost, as many municipalities produce it to recycle yard waste and sell it to residents. Homeowners compost yard waste as well. A compost pile should be included in your garden plans.

As I began to add native plants to my gardens, I discovered they did not always perform well. In the fertile soil, some of the native plants became aggressive, taking up more space than I had intended, causing other plants to decline. Switch grass (*Panicum* species) began to take over the garden. Other native plants flopped, would not stand erect. Little bluestem (*Schizachyrium scoparium*) would not stand up.

The soil-growing conditions were too good. So now, when I am designing gardens, I keep in mind which plants do not make good neighbors and put them with other aggressive plants. When I use native plants, I avoid planting them in highly fertile soils, and when top-dressing borders with compost, I spread little if any around the native plants. I have already lessened my workload.

Do not add soil amendments for a prairie reconstruction you plan to seed. Once the sprayed grass has died, mow it as close to the ground as possible and rake off the debris. You have created a perfect bed for the prairie seed. It will be able to make contact with the soil. The organic matter that remains will give the seed small nooks and crannies to fall into.

An area where the sod was removed with a sod cutter is treated a bit differently. Usually the area needs no more preparation. However, if the surface of the soil is slick and compacted, rough it up by rototilling very shallowly. Use an erosion mat if planting on a slope after seeding. Erosion mats or blankets, constructed from biodegradable materials like coir, jute, and straw, come in rolls. Follow the manufacturer's instructions for use.

Planting

Prairie seed is very expensive. You do not want any of it to blow away while seeding, and you want to be sure that you have enough to cover the area. The seed varies in size from tiny to large and can be fluffy. Divide the seed into four containers, and add twice as much damp sand as seed to each container. Mix the seed and sand thoroughly. Broadcast the mix by hand to cover the entire area four times. If you run out of seed during one run, you will have enough seed to finish that run. Change your passes from north to south to east to west to be sure all areas are covered. Do not cover the seed with any soil. Use a roller to press the seed into the ground. If your site is on a slope, use an erosion mat to prevent the seed from washing away during rain or irrigation. I have never irrigated a seeded prairie.

You may read about planting cover crops with the prairie seed. They are a quickly germinating nonnative annual plant, such as oats and winter wheat, used to hold the soil and prevent erosion and provide some shade to prevent the soil from drying out. Mow the cover crop before it forms a dense canopy or seed heads. A cover crop can provide too much shade, and it can fall over with rain and wind and smother the prairie seedlings. If you feel you need a cover crop, consult with your seed provider and describe your situation.

Plant natives grown in flats or pots in the same manner you plant nonnative perennials, shrubs, and trees. The crown of a perennial (where you see growth originating) should sit at soil level. Bring mulch up to the crown, but not over it. Dig holes for shrubs and trees slightly shallower than the height of the root ball, but twice as wide as the root ball. The depth is most important in clayey soils where the hole you dig becomes a slick pot that holds water. In these situations, rough up the sides of the hole with a fork or spade and plant high. Do not add soil amendments to the hole. Mulch up to the stems of shrubs or the trunk of trees, making sure that the mulch is not making contact with the wood.

Assess each garden's condition individually. On a site such as a newly constructed home where the soil has been stripped of topsoil and compacted by equipment, we will dig a very wide shallow hole and add compost to the backfilled soil. If I am creating a garden full of native plants on similar soil and using plugs or pots, we will rototill the beds and add compost to make the soil more hospitable to plants. In these soils, the amendments we add will not create an overly rich environment for the native plants.

Watering

All newly planted perennials, grasses, shrubs, and trees need watering the first year. This includes native plants. After the first year, native plants should not need supplemental water. However, your landscape represents a large investment in time and money. Monitor your plants for stress when temperatures are high and rainfall low: drooping and falling leaves, buds that do not open.

The most efficient watering provides water to the soil around the plants. Soaker hoses or irrigation lines with emitters target this area with very little water falling where it will quickly evaporate. Whichever system is used, cover the hose or lines with soil and mulch. For a few years I laid soaker hoses throughout my perennials beds. Eventually, I decided that spending hours moving a garden hose, attached to a spigot at the house, from garden to garden was too much. I depend on mulch, densely planted beds to shade the soil, and the Iowa rainfall that has averaged one inch a week. Two recent years of drought caused the gardens to suffer, but I lost very few plants. I water the most stressed plants with a wand or small sprinklers and very low water pressure. When I add plants, I water by hand or soaker hose the first season. During drought I notice that the native plants show less stress than the nonnatives.

For our clients we install soaker hoses in new beds and leave them in year-round. They must be disconnected from the spigot in the fall. More plants die from overwatering than underwatering. The addition of soaker hoses reassures homeowners that they can care for the beds. When homeowners leave town for a trip, they are able to instruct a friend or their house sitter how to easily water the garden. After the first year, the hoses are not needed as often. In Iowa City as in many municipalities, the cost of water is high. Conserving water and using as little as possible are main concerns. We have had problems when a client's lawn has an irrigation system and water hits the beds, drenching the leaves and the soil. The lawn emitters must be directed away from the beds.

Seeded prairies do not require watering. We seed and wait for rain. In a drought year, we have to wait longer, until the drought passes. The prairie seed waits as well. If some seed germinates and the seedlings die due to drought, we can reseed those areas. When I use small areas of low-growing, low-maintenance fescue, I instruct the clients to water that area the first season, just as they would for lawn seed.

Maintenance

I maintain gardens with a mixture of native and nonnative plants just as I would any perennial bed or mixed border of perennials and grasses. In the early spring, I cut down any perennials or grasses still standing, being sure to cut above the crown of the plant. I remove the debris, leaves, and any winter mulch, such as straw, I may have used. I compost the debris unless it shows evidence of disease, and then I burn it or put it in the trash. My compost pile does not reach the temperatures necessary to kill the organisms that cause disease. I top-dress with compost and then mulch to protect exposed soil from drying sun and wind and to suppress weeds. As noted earlier, groups of native plants need less compost, if any.

I have read articles and heard speeches about the dangers of using wood mulch. They state that it depletes forests and is not natural. In Louisiana the harvest of cypress for mulch is not sustainable. Bald cypress swamps are in decline, and cypress logging is not a sustainable operation. The shredded wood mulch I use is a by-product of the lumber industry, and using it does not deplete our forests. These forests have a natural mulch of leaf debris that gardeners try to re-create in their gardens through the use of leaf mold, compost, and wood mulch. Most of the Midwest is not treed like other parts of the United States. Our open landscape on often degraded soils needs protection provided by some kind of mulch. I would agree that wood mulch is overused and applied too deeply. Two inches are plenty, and it should be kept away from plants and the bases of trees and shrubs, where the moisture it holds will rot the bark.

One of the most tedious tasks of gardening is deadheading perennials to encourage more blooms and to maintain an attractive appearance. I do not deadhead native flowers, as I enjoy them in all seasons. I leave the spent flowers for the birds to find seeds to eat in the winter. Birds also use the garden for cover in the winter. In the fall I observe my gardens in their seasonal beauty. The leaves of the perennials and grasses turn all colors of red, yellow, orange, and brown. In late fall, I edit the garden, cutting down spent plants but leaving many to catch the snow and feed the birds in the winter.

Large areas of perennials and grasses, both native and nonnative, provide wonderful visual interest in the winter and are left standing. They also continue to provide habitat for insects and birds in late winter. In early spring, cut them down and remove the debris (as much as possible; smaller pieces will fall to the ground and improve the soil) to the compost pile. A weed whacker works well for this task. A conventional lawn mower deck cannot be set high enough.

Large-scale prairie plantings require different and greater maintenance, particularly when they are young. Many experienced restoration specialists have written on this topic. Carl Kurtz in his *Practical Guide to Prairie Reconstruction* presents concise, clear instructions. I suggest that you read this and other manuals before undertaking a substantial prairie reconstruction. Weed control ranks as the top task. Even though we rigorously remove vegetation from the site, weeds will appear. They compete with the native seedlings. On a small to medium-size residential prairie, homeowners will weed by hand. Two problems arise. One is identifying weeds and seedlings. The *Prairie Seedling and Seeding Evaluation Guide* funded by Pheasants Forever, the Minnesota Environment and Natural Resources Trust Fund, the Iowa Department of Transportation Living Roadway Trust, and other entities includes descriptions of prairie plants and weeds (seedlings and mature plants). Mark Müller drew the wonderful illustrations of the adult plants. The other problem is disturbing the soil when pulling and dislodging prairie seedlings. You may carefully use a spray bottle of herbicide on individual weeds. With a foam paintbrush, you can easily dab weeds.

For larger areas, or when high maintenance is not possible, mow the new prairie every three weeks the first year, starting when annual weed growth is twelve to fifteen inches high. Mowing will remove the tops of the weed plants before they set and drop seed. Leave enough growth to provide some shade for the seedlings. Mow to three to four inches high until the late summer, when you should mow to six to eight inches high. Most home mowers cannot be set at this height, so changing to a weed whacker works well. Also, now you can more easily avoid areas with blooming prairie plants and target weedy areas. You will need to sacrifice some flowers, but the plants' roots will continue to grow deeply into the soil. Remove debris that completely covers the plants. Smaller pieces will fall to the ground between plants. In the second season, use the weed whacker to selectively cut down weedy areas.

By the spring of the third year, there may be enough plant matter (fuel) to burn the prairie. Try to burn your prairie every three to five years. Most municipalities forbid burning or require a permit. Safety considerations are paramount. Read burning guides and consult with your fire department. Cut down the prairie every three to five years in areas where burning is forbidden or not practical. Prairie owners often rotate the areas cut or burned so they do not disturb all wildlife habitat at the same time. Burning areas of your landscape is an intimidating task. It is possible to hire people experienced in conducting burns.

Gardens are a commitment. In the planning stages, decide how much maintenance you will be able to accomplish. Plan a garden that you can manage. Are there individuals or companies available to hire to help with the work? Native plants, once established, require no more and usually less maintenance than nonnatives. Decide on your goals. Make your own design statement. I hope it will include using native plants in your garden.

Resources

Books

Armitage, Allan M. 2006. *Armitage's Native Plants for North American Gardens.* Portland, OR: Timber Press.

Brookes, John. 2008. *The Essentials of Garden Design.* New York: Alfred A. Knopf.

Burrell, C. Colston. 2006. *Native Alternatives to Invasive Plants.* New York: Brooklyn Botanic Garden.

Czarapata, Elizabeth J. 2005. *Invasive Plants of the Upper Midwest: An Illustrated Guide to Their Identification and Control.* Madison: University of Wisconsin Press.

Darke, Rick, and Doug Tallamy. 2014. *The Living Landscape for Beauty and Biodiversity in the Home Garden.* Portland, OR: Timber Press.

Diblik, Roy. 2014. *The Know Maintenance Perennial Garden.* Portland, OR: Timber Press.

Dickey, Page. 2005. *Gardens in the Spirit of Place.* New York: Stewart, Tabori and Chang.

Downing, Andrew Jackson. 1851. "A Few Hints on Landscape Gardening." In *The Native Landscape Reader,* ed. Robert E. Grese, 85–87. Amherst: University of Massachusetts Press, 2011.

Druse, Ken. 1994. *The Natural Habitat Garden.* New York: Clarkson Potter.

Grese, Robert E., ed. 2011. *The Native Landscape Reader.* Amherst: University of Massachusetts Press.

Jensen, Jens. 1906. "Landscape Art—An Inspiration from the Western Plains." In *The Native Landscape Reader*, ed. Robert E. Grese, 112–114. Amherst: University of Massachusetts Press, 2011.

———. 1920. "I Like Our Prairie Landscape." In *The Native Landscape Reader*, ed. Robert E. Grese, 102–106. Amherst: University of Massachusetts Press, 2011.

Kinsey, Joni L. 1996. *Plain Pictures: Images of the American Prairie.* Washington, DC: Smithsonian Institution Press.

Kurtz, Carl. 1996. *Iowa's Wild Places.* Ames: Iowa State University Press and the Iowa Natural Heritage Foundation.

———. 2013. *A Practical Guide to Prairie Reconstruction.* 2nd ed. Iowa City: University of Iowa Press.

Leopold, Aldo. 1926. "The Last Stand of the Wilderness." In *The Native Landscape Reader*, ed. Robert E. Grese, 271–276. Amherst: University of Massachusetts Press, 2011.

Madson, John. [1982] 2013. *Where the Sky Began.* Reprint, Iowa City: University of Iowa Press.

Manning, Richard. 1995. *Grassland: The History, Biology, Politics, and Promise of the American Prairie.* New York: Viking.

Miller, Wilhelm. 1916. "The Prairie Spirit in Landscape Gardening." In *The Native Landscape Reader*, ed. Robert E. Grese, 115–118. Amherst: University of Massachusetts Press, 2011.

Mutel, Cornelia F. 2008. *The Emerald Horizon: The History of Nature in Iowa.* Iowa City: University of Iowa Press.

Nagel, Vanessa Gardner. 2010. *Understanding Garden Design.* Portland, OR: Timber Press.

Owens-Pike, Douglas. 2013. *Beautifully Sustainable: Freeing Yourself to Enjoy Your Landscape.* Minneapolis: Be-Mondo Publishing.

Prairie Seedling and Seeding Evaluation Guide. Funded by Pheasants Forever, the Minnesota Environment and Natural Resources Trust Fund, and the Iowa Department of Transportation Living Roadway Trust et al.

Rehmann, Elsa. 1933. "An Ecological Approach." In *The Native Landscape Reader*, ed. Robert E. Grese, 157–162. Amherst: University of Massachusetts Press, 2011.

Riis, Paul B. 1937. "Ecological Garden and Arboretum at the University of

Wisconsin." In *The Native Landscape Reader*, ed. Robert E. Grese, 277–286. Amherst: University of Massachusetts Press, 2011.

Savage, Candace. 2011. *Prairie: A Natural History.* Vancouver, Canada: D&M Publishers.

Sayre, Robert, ed. 1989. *Take This Exit: Rediscovering the Iowa Landscape.* Ames: Iowa State University Press.

———, ed. 2000. *Take the Next Exit: New Views of the Iowa Landscape.* Ames: Iowa State University Press.

Smith, Daryl, Dave Williams, Greg Houseal, and Kirk Henderson. 2010. *The Tallgrass Prairie Center Guide to Prairie Restoration in the Upper Midwest.* Iowa City: University of Iowa Press.

Steiner, Lynn M. 2005. *Landscaping with Native Plants of Minnesota.* Minneapolis: Voyageur Press.

Tallamy, Douglas W. [2007] 2009. *Bringing Nature Home: How You Can Sustain Wildlife with Native Plants.* Updated and expanded ed. Reprint, Portland, OR: Timber Press.

Wasowski, Sally. 2002. *Gardening with Prairie Plants: How to Create Beautiful Native Gardens.* Minneapolis: University of Minnesota Press.

Waugh, Frank A. 1917. "The Natural Style in Landscape Gardening." In *The Native Landscape Reader*, ed. Robert E. Grese, 119–129. Amherst: University of Massachusetts Press, 2011.

Information Sources

EcoBeneficial!: www.ecobeneficial.com [horticultural communications and consulting company blog]

Johnson's Nursery: www.johnsonsnursery.com/plant_talk.cfm [Mike Yanny's blog]

Monarch Gardens: www.monarchgard.com [The Deep Middle blog on Living and Writing in the Prairie Echo]

Rainscaping Iowa: www.rainscapingiowa.org [promotes urban storm water management, publications, and workshops on rain gardens and other practices]

Sustainable Sites Initiative: www.sustainablesites.org [published a tool for guiding and measuring landscape sustainability]

Tallgrass Prairie Center: http://www.tallgrassprairiecenter.org/integrated-roadside-vegetation-mgmt/irvm-technical-manual [*Integrated Roadside Vegetation Management (IRVM) Technical Manual*]

Organizations

Association of Professional Landscape Designers: www.apld.org [find a designer]

Bur Oak Land Trust: www.buroaklandtrust.org

Ecological Landscape Alliance: www.ecolandscaping.org [sign up for newsletter]

Iowa Prairie Network: www.iowaprairienetwork.org

Midwest Ecological Landscape Alliance: www.melaweb.org [based in Illinois]

Places to Visit

Chicago Botanic Garden: www.chicagobotanic.org [visit the Dixon Prairie and Native Plant Garden, Glencoe, Illinois]

Friends of Neal Smith National Wildlife Refuge: www.tallgrass.org [Neal Smith National Wildlife Refuge offers trails to explore and educational experiences, Prairie City, Iowa]

Lurie Garden: www.luriegarden.org [Millennium Park, Chicago]

Morton Arboretum: www.mortonarb.org [visit the Schulenberg Prairie and the Wild Garden, Lisle, Illinois]

Tallgrass Prairie Center: www.tallgrassprairiecenter.org [restores native vegetation for the benefit of society and environment through research, education, and technology, Cedar Falls, Iowa]

Seed and Plant Sources

Ion Exchange, Inc., Harpers Ferry, IA: www.ionxchange.com

Johnson's Nursery, Menomonee Falls, WI: www.johnsonsnursery.com

Midwest Groundcovers, St. Charles, IL: www.midwestgroundcovers.com

Northwind Perennial Farm, Burlington, WI: www.northwindperennialfarm.com

Pizzo Native Plant Nursery, Leland, IL: www.pizzonursery.com

Prairie Moon Nursery, Winona, MN: www.prairiemoon.com

Prairie Nursery, Westfield, WI: www.prairienursery.com, www.american-natives.com

Index

diversity, 5; botanical, 23; ecological, 54; in the garden, 19–20, 22; genetic, 66; wildlife, 15

Downing, Andrew Jackson, 18

Dropmore catmint (*Nepeta* 'Dropmore'), 69

drought, 85, 115

eastern cottonwood (*Populus deltoides*), 38

eastern redbud (*Cercis canadensis*), 20

EcoBeneficial, 19

Ecological Garden and Arboretum at the University of Wisconsin, 27

ecologists, 2, 111

ecology, 27; environmental, defined, 22; plant, 26

ecosystem, 2, 14, 112

ecosystem services, 20

ecotype, defined, 64

Eierman, Kim, 19, 21–23

The Emerald Horizon (Mutel), 13

Energyscapes, 48

entry gardens, 37–38, 78. *See also* gardens

environment, 5, 19, 26, 67, 71, 114; damaged, 7; diverse, 25

erosion, 84, 114; mat, 85, 113

evening primrose (*Oenothera biennis*), 90

exotics. *See* plants

explorers, 10; French, 10; and settlers, 10–11

extinction, 26

false blue indigo (*Baptisia australis*), 42, 67

fernleaf yarrow (*Achillea filipendulina*), 54

fescue, 115. *See also* seed

fire, 13. *See also* burning

flats, 114; defined, 63

flat-topped aster (*Doellingeria umbellata*), 73

Flower, George, 10

foundation plantings, 56–58, 76, 113–114

foxglove beardtongue (*Penstemon digitalis*), 78, 88, 92

gardens: backyard, 38–2; deer-resistant, 67, 76; defined, 30; designers, 6; naturalistic, 38; shade, 56; traditional, 38. *See also* beds and borders; deer population; entry gardens; maintenance; paths; patios; ponds; rain garden

Gardens in the Spirit of Place (Dickey), 66

genetic diversity, 66. *See also* diversity

genotype, defined, 66

geology and climate, 12–14

glaciations, 12; glaciers, 12–13

glossy buckthorn (*Rhamnus frangula*), 92

glyphosate, 84, 92, 101, 110–111

golden alexander (*Zizia aurea*), 48

Golden Glory cornelian cherry dogwood (*Cornus mas* 'Golden Glory'), 80

Golden Showers coreopsis (*Coreopsis verticillata* 'Golden Showers'), 71–72

Golden Spirit smokebush (*Cotinus coggygria* 'Golden Spirit'), 80

goldenrod (*Solidago* species), 100

Goldsturm black-eyed Susan (*Rudbeckia fulgida* 'Goldsturm'), 3, 42, 54, 78

Gold Dew tufted hair grass (*Deschampsia* 'Goldtau'), 69–70

grassland, 10, 11, 13

gray-headed coneflower (*Ratibida pinnata*), 41–42, 94, 99

Grese, Robert, 17, 27

Groat, Debbie, 56

maintenance, 53, 85, 109, 116–118; low, 80

May Night salvia (*Salvia nemorosa* 'Mainacht'), 42

mayapple (*Podophyllum peltatum*), 102

meadow, defined, 10

Michigan, 11, 12

milkweed (*Asclepias* species), 26

Miller, Wilhem, 12

Minnesota, 11, 48

Minnesota Environment and Natural Resources Trust Fund, 117

Mississippi River, 10, 13

Missouri, 11; St. Louis, 73

Missouri River, 13

Moerheim Beauty sneezeweed (*Helenium* 'Moerheim Beauty'), 73–74

Monarch butterfly, 26

moonshine yarrow (*Achillea millifolium* 'Moonshine'), 78

mountain mint (*Pycnanthemum* species), 105

mulch, 47, 114, 115; cypress, 116; sustainable, 116; wood, 116

Müller, Mark, 95, 117

Mutel, Cornelia F., 1, 13–14, 22, 104

Mutel, Robert, 104

Nagel, Vanessa, 36

nativar, defined, 64; 65–66

Native Alternatives to Invasive Plants (Burrell), 24

Native Americans, 11, 13

native cultivar, 64–66

The Native Landscape Reader (Grese), 17, 27

native plants, 1–5; defined, 2; in gardens, 5–7

native species, defined, 1

natural landscape. *See* landscape

Natural Selection Seed at the Tallgrass Prairie Center of Northern Iowa

natural world, 9

naturalistic style, 68. *See also* landscape and gardens

Nebraska, 11

New England aster (*Symphyotrichum novae-angliae*), 4

New York City, 38

No Mow Lawn Seed Mix, Prairie Nursery, 48, 95

No-Mow/Low-Grow Lawn Seed, Ion Exchange, 86

northern sea oats (*Chasmanthium latifolium*), 32, 88–89

Northwind Perennial Farm, 68

Northwind switch grass (*Panicum virgatum* 'Northwind'), 65, 72–73, 78

obedient plant (*Physostegia virginiana*), 56

Oceanarium, Chicago Shedd Aquarium, 68

Ohio, 12, 38, 60; Akron, 95

ornamental onion (*Allium* species), 76

Oudolf, Piet, 38

oxeye false sunflower (*Heliopsis helianthoides*), 19

pagoda dogwood (*Cornus alternifolia*), 56–57

pale purple coneflower (*Echinacea pallida*), 42, 58, 67, 92, 95

partridge pea (*Chamaecrista fasciculata*), 98

paths, 50–53

patios, 91, 105

peat, 112

peony (*Paeonia* species), 61

Peter Pan goldenrod (*Solidago* 'Peter Pan'), 3, 80

Pixie Meadowbrite coneflower (*Echinacea* 'Pixie Meadowbrite'), 72

Pizzo, Jack, 2, 19, 104–105

Pizzo Associates, 55, 104

Pizzo Native Plant Nursery, 104

BUR OAK GUIDES

The Butterflies of Iowa
Dennis W. Schlicht, John C. Downey, and Jeffrey C. Nekola

A Country So Full of Game: The Story of Wildlife in Iowa
James J. Dinsmore

The Emerald Horizon: The History of Nature in Iowa
Cornelia F. Mutel

Field Guide to Wildflowers of Nebraska and the Great Plains
Jon Farrar

Forest and Shade Trees of Iowa
Peter J. van der Linden and Donald R. Farrar

Grasses in Your Pocket: A Guide to the Prairie Grasses of the Upper Midwest
Anna B. Gardner, Michael Hurst, Deborah Lewis, and Lynn G. Clark

The Guide to Oklahoma Wildflowers
Patricia Folley

An Illustrated Guide to Iowa Prairie Plants
Paul Christiansen and Mark Müller

Landforms of Iowa
Jean C. Prior

Mushrooms and Other Fungi of the Midcontinental United States
D. M. Huffman, L. H. Tiffany, G. Knaphus, and R. A. Healy

A Practical Guide to Prairie Restoration
Carl Kurtz

Prairie: A North American Guide
Suzanne Winckler

Prairie in Your Pocket: A Guide to Plants of the Tallgrass Prairie
Mark Müller

The Tallgrass Prairie Center Guide to Prairie Restoration in the Upper Midwest
Daryl Smith, Dave Williams, Greg Houseal, and Kirk Henderson

The Tallgrass Prairie Center Guide to Seed and Seedling Identification in the Upper Midwest
Dave Williams and Brent Butler

The Tallgrass Prairie Reader
John T. Price

Trees in Your Pocket: A Guide to Trees of the Upper Midwest
Thomas Rosburg

The Vascular Plants of Iowa: An Annotated Checklist and Natural History
Lawrence J. Eilers and Dean M. Roosa

Wetlands in Your Pocket: A Guide to Common Plants and Animals of Midwestern Wetlands
Mark Müller

Where the Sky Began: Land of the Tallgrass Prairie
John Madson

Wildflowers and Other Plants of Iowa Wetlands
Sylvan T. Runkel and Dean M. Roosa

Wildflowers of Iowa Woodlands
Sylvan T. Runkel and Alvin F. Bull

Wildflowers of the Tallgrass Prairie: The Upper Midwest
Sylvan T. Runkel and Dean M. Roosa

Woodland in Your Pocket: A Guide to Common Woodland Plants of the Midwest
Mark Müller